HOPE IS RISING
Stories of Transformed Lives in the Coachella Valley

Published in Beaverton, Oregon, by Good Catch Publishing.
www.goodcatchpublishing.com
V1.1

Printed in the United States of America

Table of Contents

Dedication   9

Acknowledgements   11

Introduction   15

1 Cosmic Comfort   17

2 Cusp of the Grave   39

3 Journey Out of Pain   65

4 New Beginnings   91

5 The Road of Endurance   117

6 The Long Road Home   157

7 Unresolved   183

Conclusion   205

DEDICATION

We would like to thank the hundreds of people who submitted their personal life story for this book and those who have financially given to make this book possible. This has been an amazing group effort from some amazing people!

We also give a special thank you to the eight people who have graciously allowed us to put their stories in this book. Your courage and boldness will bring hope to many people in our valley. Thank you for making this city your life.

We dedicate this book to the people who live in the Coachella Valley. It is our hope that as you read these real-life stories you will find the hope, direction and answers you need.

ACKNOWLEDGEMENTS

I would like to thank Eddie Windsor for his vision for this book and Ryan Lovett for his hard work in making it a reality. And to the people of Champion Life, thank you for your boldness and vulnerability in sharing your personal stories.

This book would not have been published without the amazing efforts of our project manager and editor, Hayley Pandolph. Her untiring resolve pushed this project forward and turned it into a stunning victory. Thank you for your great fortitude and diligence. Deep thanks to our incredible editor in chief, Michelle Cuthrell, and executive editor, Jen Genovesi, for all the amazing work they do. I would also like to thank our invaluable proofreader, Melody Davis, for the focus and energy she has put into perfecting our words.

Lastly, I want to extend our gratitude to the creative and very talented Jenny Randle, who designed the beautiful cover for *Hope is Rising: Stories of Transformed Lives in the Coachella Valley.*

Daren Lindley
President and CEO
Good Catch Publishing

The book you are about to read
is a compilation of authentic life stories.
The facts are true, and the events are real.
These storytellers have dealt with crisis, tragedy, abuse
and neglect and have shared their most private moments,
mess-ups and hang-ups in order for others to learn and
grow from them. In order to protect the identities of those
involved in their pasts, the names and details of some
storytellers have been withheld or changed.

INTRODUCTION

If you had to tell someone the story of your life, what kind of story would it be? Would it be a picturesque all-American tale of love and success? Would it be riddled with lies, deception and corruption? Would you shy away from the embarrassing or haunting facts that created turmoil and destruction in your journey?

The stories you are about to read are actual happenings in the lives of people in our own Coachella Valley. Some take you down dark paths of addiction and depression, while others admit to overwhelming fear and abuse. These kinds of stories are very difficult to tell ... and to read. However, they all have one common denominator that drastically changed the course of their lives.

In these pages you will be taken on eight different journeys that will ultimately reveal their source of hope and change. You may be able to relate to the darkness in these situations; if so, our hope is that you will realize there is a purpose for your life, and there is more to life than you're currently experiencing. There is a life that you can live that is big and full, contrary to what most people think is even possible. As you read these stories, you will find that hope and greatness can arise in your life as well.

COSMIC COMFORT
The Story of Joshua
Written by Arlene Showalter

I rolled out of bed, rubbing my aching head. Another night of drugs, sex and booze had failed again to erase the unhappy truth. *He's really gone. Dad's still dead.*

I picked up my cell phone to check the time. Dozens of missed calls, all from my brother's best friend. Worry chewed at my gut as I called him back.

"What's up?" I asked, stretching one arm over my head and cradling the phone with the other.

"Will didn't make it. He's dead."

ॐॐॐ

"Keep your eye on the ball, son."

I grinned. Dad, my best friend, coached me from the sidelines. I listened and obeyed.

My bat connected with the ball. *Thwack.*

"Run, Josh, run!" Dad shouted.

He's the best, I thought, as I tagged first base and slid into second.

Mom and Dad produced four kids in five years. I sat at the bottom in birth order but the top in Dad's heart. We were inseparable.

He owned a pawn shop, and Mom taught at our

school. We all went to church and lived normal, secure, contented lives.

"Where's Daddy?" I asked one day when he failed to appear for dinner.

"Daddy got in trouble today." Mom looked around the table until her eyes settled on me. Somehow I knew she had something important to say.

"How?" 12-year-old Will asked.

"His partner brought in hot goods that your dad sold."

"Hot?" I asked. "How come he touched hot stuff?"

"Hot means stolen," Will said. He turned back to Mom. "Did Dad know they were hot?"

"No, but the cops took him in, anyway."

"Why?" I asked.

"As far as the law is concerned, Dad owns the shop, so he's responsible. He's staying in jail now, until he's sentenced."

"What's jail? What's sin-tanced?"

"It's a place where people who break the law have to stay. Honey, he has to stand in front of a man called a judge. The judge decides how long he has to go to prison." She pushed her untouched food around in circles on her plate. "Selling stolen items is an automatic two to three years."

Two or three years? My mind spun like a released top. "You mean he won't be back until I'm 9 — or 10?"

"I'm sorry, Josh." Mom leaned over to hug my shaking shoulders.

"It's going to be hard on all of us. We'll all have to help each other get through it."

"I miss Daddy," I sniveled, a few nights later, in the room I shared with my two older brothers, Will and Sam.

"Come over here." Will threw back his covers. "You can sleep with me."

I snuggled down against him.

"I miss Daddy," I repeated. "How can I wait so long to see him?"

Will wrapped his arms around me. "I know it seems like forever when you're little, but the time will go fast. You'll see." He rubbed my head. "I miss him, too. Don't worry, kid, everything will be okay."

"I want to draw him a picture," I said, popping up.

"That's a great idea."

"Every day."

"Even better."

"I want Daddy to know I love him so much."

ॐॐॐ

Life turned down Hard-Times Lane after Dad left. Of course, we lost his income, and it was tough with four children. People felt sorry for us and donated food.

Mom left teaching to work at a real estate management company in an effort to make more money to support us. But what hurt more than the loss of Dad's money was the huge hole his absence left in my life and heart.

❧❧❧

"Where's Mom?" I asked 10-year-old Sam, a year later.

"Dunno." His eyes never left the TV.

I searched our three-bedroom apartment. Every bedroom empty. I peeked in my parents' bedroom. No Mom, but I heard a faint murmuring. *Where's it coming from?* I tiptoed in the room, listening. Eventually, I came to the closed closet door and pressed an ear against it. *Mommy!*

I opened the door. She knelt beneath Dad's shirts.

"What are you doing?"

"Talking to God."

"How come you hafta talk to God in here?"

Her dark eyes mirrored deep sadness.

"I can concentrate better."

Her answer seemed silly. I shrugged and left.

❧❧❧

Dad finally returned. Joy ran amok, but so did fear. *What if he leaves again?*

"What's wrong, buddy?" Dad asked me on countless nights. I remained silent as the tears rolled from my eyes.

How can I tell him how afraid I am that he's gonna leave me again? I just sobbed. Night after night, Dad gathered me in his arms until I fell asleep.

He began helping Mom with maintenance for the complex she managed. Life settled into the normal routine I cherished. Then Dad returned to a false comforter, one he'd known in his younger days — speed — setting a devastating pattern that lasted the next 10 years in our home: Work hard, coach baseball, chase speed, return to prison, come home, work hard, chase speed until arrested and start the vicious cycle again.

I wept alone the nights he was gone and in his arms the nights when he came back. We always knew when he was out pursuing speed because he'd disappear for several days. When that happened, I'd grab my skateboard and cruise the town until I located his work van.

"Come on home, Dad," I begged.

"Later, son."

"Why?"

"I'll be okay," he said. "I'll come later."

I went home and told Mom.

"I found Dad and asked him to come home."

"No." Her tone and eyes sharpened. "I'll not have him under this roof in that condition."

"Please, Mom? He's my dad."

"No."

But, sometimes, with a lot of pleading, her *no* turned to *yes*. Those times, I raced back and told Dad.

☙☙☙

"Your father's gone again," Mom announced when I was 10.

"Why?" My greatest fear tore at me like buzzards on a carcass.

"You know why."

"Busted again? How long this time?"

"Two years."

"I have to write to him," I said, sitting down at the kitchen table. "Every day. He has to know how much I love him."

Once a week, Dad called from prison. We chatted for a few minutes.

"I wish you were here."

"So do I, son."

"Here's Will." I handed the phone off and went to my room to wrap myself in my own misery.

As the eldest son, Will tried to fill Dad's shoes, and Mom tried to be father and mother to us all. Life plodded on toward the next release date, strung together by letters and phone calls.

Dad came home. He returned to coaching my baseball team, then he got busted again.

I can't take it. The emptiness. The stares of my teammates.

I quit the team. Dad served his time and came back.

"You're old enough to help me on the job," Dad announced when I was 15. "I'll teach you basic maintenance skills."

"Super."

"Okay, son. Watch and learn."

One weekend he asked, "Want to ride over to your grandparents? I'll show you how to paint."

"Sure!"

We loaded up Dad's van with paint and brushes and left for the hour-long drive. Just as Dad turned the van onto the freeway, we passed a homeless man walking on the side of the road.

"Hey, Dad, see that dude?"

Dad glanced in the rearview mirror and grunted.

"You're gonna turn out just like that if you don't stop screwing around."

He gave me a strange look, but kept silent.

෬෬෬

My brothers quickly built reputations in school as crazy guys not to be messed with. They thrived on the violence, and by the time I entered the same high school, I matched them, fist for fist.

I discovered an outlet for the pain of disappointment and my dad's frequent disappearing and reappearing acts. I discovered girls and quickly learned to use them to my own advantage. I started to party hard — drinking, experimenting with weed and hooking up with lots of girls.

෬෬෬

I loved my dad, but I admired my mom. *She is such an amazing woman. She stands by Dad no matter how much he messes up.*

Every time Dad came back, I thought, *Maybe this time he'll get it right and straighten out.*

We shot rockets in the desert, played basketball and walked Grandma's dogs together. Then he disappeared. Again. I knew the routine. I set out to find him.

One night, when I was 14, Sam and I sat watching the local news together. Suddenly a familiar blue van flashed on the screen.

"That looks like Dad's work van," I said.

"What's going on?" Sam straightened up to lean toward the TV.

"There's a rag stuffed in the gas tank," I gasped as the camera zoomed in and then back out. We saw Dad shuffling around, talking to the police.

We sat in stupefied silence as the TV reporter intoned about a standoff between our parents where Mom worked.

"You've got to be kidding," Sam said. "What the h*** is going on?"

Mom called us, a few hours later, from work.

"Your dad came to my work today," she said, "high on drugs and itching for a fight. He threatened to blow up his van, so I called the police."

"What are the charges this time?" I asked.

"Disturbing the peace, resisting arrest and assaulting an officer."

Dad returned to prison.

Here we go again.

COSMIC COMFORT

వ్యావ్యావ్యా

Not long after that, I was looking for something in Mom's bedroom. I saw a letter addressed to Dad on her dresser. I pulled the letter out of the envelope and smoothed the single page.

I can't live like this any longer, she wrote. *I'm getting remarried, because I finally realize you'll never change.*

They're getting divorced? Anger exploded. *She can't take my dad away from me.*

After 25 years of marriage — 14 of which Mom lived as a single parent while Dad served various sentences — she divorced Dad and announced she was going to marry Henry, a man we'd recently met.

"I can't believe she's doing this to us," I complained to my brothers.

"What's wrong with you?" Will demanded. "Mom's put up with Dad's s*** all these years. You need to man up and let her get on with life. She deserves to be happy."

"Dad will change. She should give him another chance."

"Yeah, right." Will snorted. "He'll change just like he has all the other times." He glared at me. "Let Mom have a little joy in her life."

"Then why can't she wait until I get out of high school?" I asked.

"It's not about you. Stop being so selfish."

"How're you doing?" Aunt Sue asked at the wedding.

"I don't like him." I scowled at Mom and Henry sharing a laugh over the wedding cake. "I don't even know him. How could she do this to me?"

Because I was the only kid still at home, I had to leave the only place I'd ever lived and move with Mom into a new house with Henry.

Mom cut off all communication with Dad. "I don't want him to know where we live and cause trouble."

I balled my fists and stomped from the room. *I'll man up like my brothers want and stop whining about life.*

Will became even more important to me. I emulated his behavior and habits. We experimented with various drugs together. I learned to fight as fiercely as he.

We attended a party together when I was 17. I pursued my new pain-deadening hobbies: screwing girls, drinking and drugs. Will and his best friend started fighting. I grabbed my empty beer bottle and smashed it in the other guy's face.

I yawned in class the next day. The fight from the night before felt as relevant as the history teacher's lecture. A kid came into the room and handed him a slip of paper.

"Josh, you're wanted in the principal's office."

What for?

I entered the room. Two policemen faced me.

"Do you know why you're here?" one asked, while the other slipped behind me.

"Uh-uh."

"Attempted murder. Please put your hands behind your back."

What?

"You were at a party last night?"

"Yes."

"And got into a fight?"

I nodded.

"You know how much damage you did to that kid?"

"Nope." I shrugged. "Kid has a potty mouth."

"Doctors say it'll take 30 grand to repair your work."

The cops released me into Mom's custody. I have no idea why, but later, the guy's parents dropped all charges.

❧❧❧

"Check this out." Scott, my best friend, held something out as he drove us to school.

"What is it?"

"Just try it."

I pinched one nostril shut and sniffed.

Comfort — amazing, soothing, calming comfort spread through my body. "Wow. Good stuff."

"Got lots where that came from."

Scott worked at a local golf course. We started skipping classes to indulge in our new love affair with Madame Cocaine.

"What the h*** you doing?" Will screamed. "Mom told me about you playing hooky and snorting. You're screwing up your life."

Shut up, you b******, I wanted to scream back. *You took Mom's side in the divorce. I'll never forgive you for turning your back on Dad.*

Instead, I shrugged.

৵৵৵

Dad was diagnosed with Hepatitis C during his last incarceration. After he served his time, he moved into a halfway house. His lungs began filling with fluid and had to be drained every week.

Will had joined the Navy and was stationed in Tacoma, Washington, but he returned to help my dad.

I'd quit school and started working in the family business. One uncle called me soon after my dad's move.

"Your dad's really sick. He's in the hospital."

I went to visit him. He looked bad, lying there with a breathing tube stuck in his nose, but I felt no real concern.

He's a tough bird. He's been in worse messes than this. He'll be okay.

I left and resumed my life of booze, sex and coke.

A few days later, Dad called me.

"I need money to pay my buddy for that transmission he's rebuilding for you."

"Okay, Dad, okay. I'm busy right now. I'll get the money to you next week. Don't blow a gasket about it." I flipped my cell phone shut and shoved it in my pocket.

The next day another uncle called — one who'd never, ever called me before.

This can't be good, I thought as I punched the answer button.

"Hey, Nick. What's up?"

"Your dad's gone."

Gone? Dad's always been "gone" for us. He'll be back. It'll be okay.

"Do you understand?" he asked. "He died."

It took years for me to realize that this time Dad would never return.

The funeral passed in a haze of shock, grief and resentment. *How can this be happening?*

∂∘∂∘∂∘

"Josh, I need your help." Don called four days after Dad's funeral. "Your brother wants to fight me. Over Samantha." Samantha bounced back and forth from Don to Will. At the moment she was back with Don.

"I don't want to fight him. He's threatened to kill me."

"My brother talks a tough game." I laughed. "But that's all it is — talk."

"Can't you talk him out of this?" Don begged.

"You've got nothing to worry about. I know my brother. He couldn't kill anybody."

Will did beat up Don. He didn't kill him.

Five days later, Will and I partied hard with coke and ran about looking for trouble. Trouble found Will two days later.

"Don is beating up Samantha." Will called me around

4 a.m. on his cell phone. "I'm driving to Hollywood to pick her up."

"Hey, man, I gotta get some sleep. Can you just wait until morning? I'll go with you then."

"Okay. I'll wait."

I dropped into bed, still under the influence of drugs, booze, sex and grief over my father's death.

A few hours later, the phone rang again.

"Ugh," I groaned. "Who's calling at 7 in the morning? Hello?"

"Josh, this is Samantha. Will's been stabbed really bad," she said, sobbing. "I don't think he's going to make it."

"Relax, Samantha. I've seen Will be shot before. And stabbed. He's tough. He'll make it. Don't worry."

I fell back on my pillow and was asleep in minutes.

I woke up hours later, rubbing my eyes with a groan. I picked up my cell phone and gasped.

Thirty-two missed calls. All from Will's best friend, Carl. I punched the return call button. Before Carl could respond, I blurted out, "What's up?"

"He's gone." Carl choked. "Will's dead."

"What do you mean? What happened?"

"Don wasted him."

"How?"

"Will beat him up again. When he started walking away, Don jumped up and stabbed him in the back. Four times."

Time froze.

He can't be gone. Not Will. Nobody bests Will. Ever.

"He turned around," Carl continued, "and Don stabbed him once in the front. Pierced his heart."

I hung up without saying goodbye. For hours, I stared at nothing, trying to digest Carl's news. Will, like Dad, would never return.

Later that day I went in search of my drug contacts.

"I need some OxyContin — now." Will and I sold it ourselves, but didn't use it.

"You'll be hooked the first time you try it," he had cautioned.

"I won't touch it," I promised.

Today was different.

Dad is dead. Now Will, my other hero, is dead. I need to be dead, too.

OxyContin got me through Will's funeral, dry-eyed and tight-lipped. In the days that followed, I used, abused and craved more. Life held no meaning. No future. No interest.

I pursued both OxyContin and her twin, heroin, with greater determination than weed, coke or sex. I sold OxyContin, but she owned me. *I don't care about tomorrow, I just need to be all right for now.*

"I can't watch you kill yourself," Mom said when my weight dropped 40 pounds. "I watched your dad go this route, and I can't do it again."

I shrugged.

"Henry and I are moving out."

"This is Henry's house."

"We don't want you to be homeless, and I can't watch you kill yourself, so we're leaving."

Whatever.

"Josh," Mom whispered.

I turned around. I recognized that look in her eyes. The same as when I found her praying in the closet years back. "You really should give God a chance. He's the only one who can truly help you in your pain."

Yeah, right. Lot of good he's done so far, letting Dad and Will die. I'll never seek his help — ever.

My family begged me to go into rehab and offered to pay the expenses. I went but couldn't handle the emotional pain. I snorted heroin during my stay and returned to full-time usage almost as soon as I got released.

আ⁓আ⁓আ

Orange construction-zone cones zipped past my window as I sped down the highway and wrestled with myself. My thoughts turned to an unwelcome God. Mom and Amelia, my friend Rick's sister, had tried to get me to turn to God so often. Rick, who had lived as wildly as I and ran in the same circles, decided to become a God-follower and seemed to be pretty genuine about it.

"He can show you the way to straighten out your life," he told me.

"Why should I trust God? He didn't help Dad get his act together so he could come back and live with us permanently. He didn't stop Mom's divorce or remarriage."

"I don't pretend to know why God lets bad things happen," Rick replied. "But I do know he's big enough to help you change your life."

I didn't know what to think about all that as I drove faster and faster down the highway. All I felt was anger. "Wasn't Dad's death enough for you?" I yelled out loud as I gripped the steering wheel of my beat-up clunker. I'd traded the nice car Dad had left me for a mere $50 worth of heroin.

"You had to go and let Will get killed and leave us, too? How can you be this good God that Mom and Rick always blab about?"

The cones flew by faster.

"You don't care about me or the crappy way I grew up — always waiting for Dad to come home. I'll keep using because I'm never going to trust you. Ever. I have nothing to live for but everything to die for. Man, all I have to do right now is hit that concrete barrier, and it's all over. You'll never hurt me again."

I had heroin in my system and my pocket as I hurtled down the highway. She'd been my faithful mistress for three years, but now she failed to deliver that familiar comfort.

I punched the accelerator and focused on the concrete road divider ahead.

I'll be dead in an instant, and then everything will be fine.

Suddenly, words erupted from my mouth. Unexpected, un-thought-out cries.

"God, you're gonna hafta show up right now because I don't know what to do. I'm done!"

In that moment, an unfamiliar peace settled over me while all thoughts of self-annihilation flew out the window. I slowed the car, maintained my lane and drove home.

"I'm ready to go back to rehab," I announced. "I can't do this anymore."

❧❧❧

"You need to surrender your life," an ex-con in the facility told me.

"I can give up the drugs," I said, "and the sex and booze. I'll do it on my own."

"You'll fail without God's help."

"He's never been there for me. Either he doesn't care, or he doesn't understand. Same difference."

"Why don't you write him a letter?"

"You're kidding. Write God a letter. For what?"

"Getting your thoughts on paper will help you."

I am not giving you credit for anything I accomplish here, God, I thought as I sat down to carry out the man's insane suggestion.

But I began to feel that same peace that came over me in the car and decided to get in touch with Rick.

"I need help."

"Come to church with me when you get out," he said. "It's an hour from you, but it will be well worth the drive."

"Okay, I'll do it."

෯෯෯

The moment I walked into the church, that same presence filled me again.

This is the same feeling I had in the car, when I wanted to waste myself. It must be God.

"Anyone who feels he or she needs to get right with God," the pastor said at the end of his message, "please come to the front so I can pray with you."

"God, I need your help," I prayed as I walked forward. "I've made a real mess of things. I've used women. I've used drugs for years and beat up more people than I can count."

My dad's face floated into my thoughts. "Look how badly I treated Dad when he was dying. The last words he ever heard from me were cruel and selfish."

Henry's face appeared next. The horrible, disrespectful way I'd treated him since he married Mom. How I put Will off when I wanted some sleep and never saw him alive again. The real me became painfully clear. I recoiled in disgust.

"I love you, Josh. I'm here to save you from yourself." I seemed to hear God's voice in the deepest part of me.

"I've always been with you, son. Even in all the pain of your life. Even when you tried to run away and ignore my existence. I've been waiting for you to come back to me so I can heal your wounds."

Peace — a genuine, solid comfort — settled into my being as I realized that God accepted me, as is. Gratitude swept over me as I stopped fighting God and accepted him.

"From now on, God, I'm letting you run my life."

A week later, the church held a baptism service. I got baptized, determined to show everyone who knew me that the old Josh was gone, dead and buried, and a new Josh would live out his days living for Jesus.

Rick and I enjoyed the church in Corona, but we both felt we needed to find a church closer to home.

"Let's pray that God will guide us to a good church in our valley," I said.

"Hey, dude."

Rick called me a few weeks later. "I heard about a church over in Palm Desert called Champion Life Church. Want to try it?"

"Sure. Twenty minutes is better than an hour."

We went to Champion Life Church together. The moment I walked in, I felt God's presence again, the same as I'd felt in the car moments before I scrapped the suicide idea. God's love shone through the faces and in the words of the people who surrounded me.

"What's your name? How are you?"

These people don't know me or what I've done, but I feel the honesty in their voices.

Rick and I sat down. Again, God's comforting presence surrounded me as the worship team began. The real deal, not the temporary solace I got from heroin.

I want to be a part of this place. God is obviously really important in these people's lives. They're really trying to live for God. I need that encouragement. I want to be around people like that and live like that.

❧❧❧

One day, our pastor invited me to lunch. *This man really wants to know me. He really cares.*

Then he challenged me.

"There is a generation being awakened by God," he said. "Champion Life is about people. Authentic and passionate people who have joined together to embrace a cause bigger than ourselves. We are a community and people dedicated to making a difference here at home and abroad. You want to be a part of it, Josh?"

I didn't even hesitate.

"I do. I want to tell *everybody* how I owe my very life to God's goodness."

CUSP OF THE GRAVE
The Story of Samuel
Written by Douglas Abbott

They were there to kill me. There were 10 of them, armed with clubs and chains, completely surrounding me. Even if I could slip away from them, they knew where I lived. But even running was impossible. They had two dogs on leashes, both of them itching to sink their teeth into me. There was no way out of this.

The only thing that could turn this around was for me to produce thousands of dollars to replace what had been stolen from them.

But I didn't have it. The men responsible for this were long gone, and I had been left holding the bag.

"Are you ready to die, motherf*****?" the leader asked. His chain rattled, and I thought I could see a few crimson stains on the links. Suddenly I saw myself on the ground, a mass of torn flesh and splintered bones. I could almost hear the meaty crunch as their clubs hit the broken body on the concrete. My body.

I was going to die. And truth be told, it was exactly what I deserved.

❧❧❧

When I was growing up, I didn't know who or what I was supposed to be. Religion was my family's business. My father was a preacher, as was my grandfather, my great-grandfather and my great-great-grandfather. Whatever I needed from religion, I thought I had it by virtue of my lineage. I had no desire to approach God or to step into a pastoral role, and yet I felt I was under incredible pressure to do so.

I grew up knowing I was loved and supported by my parents. However, I couldn't help noticing that they were always away at the church with the youth group. I had the undeniable feeling that my parents considered their church flock more important than me. I suspected the reason was that I wasn't good enough to fit into the family niche, which was all about going to church and doing acts of service, neither of which interested me much. We were constantly traveling and enduring hardship.

I grew up in the state of Washington, where we lived on my paternal grandparents' 450-acre farm. We had hundreds of sheep and cattle, which my sister and I often helped to care for. By the time I was 8, I was able to lift 90-pound hay bales from the baler. I loved exploring the natural environment. Whenever I got the opportunity, I made off for the woods, where I hunted and fished.

Up until I was 16, I was under 5 feet tall and weighed less than 100 pounds. This made me the object of personal attacks at school. I became an angry young man, on the edge of physical violence much of the time. I regularly flew into a rage and fought with schoolmates. I harbored anger against bullies of all kinds because of my personal experiences. In my mind, most authority figures were bullies with titles. This conviction stemmed in large part from an experience with my elementary school principal, Mr. Crowell.

My best friend and I ended up in Mr. Crowell's office after fighting on school grounds. As punishment, the principal hit me with a two-by-four hard enough to send me flying across the room and into the wall. He then repeated the procedure.

Several days later, my father noticed the marks on my backside and asked me what had happened. When I told him, he drove immediately to the school and told the principal never to touch me again, that what he had done was wrong and unacceptable. Mr. Crowell never so much as looked at me again.

છ્ર•છ્ર•છ્ર

"We're moving to England," my father announced one morning when I was 13. I was put out, although to be fair, my parents had asked both me and my sister to listen to the voice of God in the matter. However, I heard nothing. At first I thought it would be cool to move to England. However, once I was there, I was angry about being uprooted and hauled across the world. Things got worse when we ran out of money a year later. All of a sudden, we lived in hotel rooms, ate peanut butter and jelly sandwiches and green apples and spent each evening in a strange church. My father's work had us driving all over England and Wales for the next few years.

By the time I was preparing to start my senior year of high school, my parents decided to move my sister and me back to the United States. Meanwhile, my parents flew back and forth as my father continued his ministry. For the first time in my life, I was free from constant supervision. My parents spent as much as a month at a time overseas. My sister and I had the run of the house in Washington while they were gone.

Not long after I returned from England, I started sprouting up in height and developed a stocky build, which, ironically, created even more conflict between me and other young men.

I was nearly always in the mood to scrap. I even fought at church. I had two friends, Bill and Alan, who entertained themselves by running afoul of the law. We went around stealing street signs and causing a general commotion wherever we went. The three of us attended church partly out of habit and partly for the social activity it afforded.

One day I was walking with Bill and Alan through the foyer of the church just after a service. As we made our way past clusters of people, I heard a young man say, "Look at this white motherf***** thinkin' he's all bad and s***." The voice was low and filled with contempt. I looked over and saw the person who had spoken. It was a large black youth, perhaps a year or two older than I, sitting with his friends and glaring back at me. I stopped, turned and uttered a racial slur.

His eyes narrowed. "What did you call me?"

I repeated the slur. By this time, I was fully expecting a fight. My chest was thrown out, and my hands were half clenched.

"You can't talk to me that way. I know who your dad is."

"I don't care who my dad is," I said, nearly yelling.

The taunts went in both directions for a couple of minutes. Then he leaned back in his chair with a smirk on his face. Without thinking, I stepped in and kicked at one of the raised legs of his chair. As he landed smartly on the floor, I hopped over the upturned chair and began hitting him in the face as fast and hard as I could, screaming curses at him. Before long, he was unconscious. By this time, Bill and Alan were furiously at work on his friends. I looked up and discovered that we were surrounded by teenage gawkers. In the crowd, I spotted many of the same faces I had encountered at teenage parties we had attended. Most of them didn't seem to mind the violence any more than I did.

A great deal of my anger was directed at other races. I had many bad experiences. I honestly felt that my hostility toward other races was entirely defensive in origin and hence justified. Because I had been so badly bullied by people, I took out my anger on those I felt were most responsible.

Between my parents' frequent absences, my growing freedom and exposure to secular society, I had begun to change profoundly. Where before my social circle had almost entirely consisted of churchgoers, it now consisted mainly of young adults whose recreation included sex, drinking and drug use.

Around this time, I met Hannah, who was just like me, a drinker and a party animal. She was an atheist. We drank at the parties we attended, not because we had any great fondness for alcohol, but because it was fun. Soon we tried marijuana, as well.

For as long as I can remember, I have been a sensation seeker. I drove tractors and other farm vehicles while I was still so little that I had to climb up and down to alternate between steering and working the pedals. I operated backhoes, bulldozers, dump trucks, bobcats, chain saws and other types of farm equipment and vehicles. I regularly made use of the farm ATV and learned how to deactivate the governor so I could ride it at high speeds once I was out of sight of the adults. I figured trying marijuana was inevitable.

However, my first spin with drugs was an enlightening experience. Hannah and I attended a party where 50 young people spent the evening getting high and drunk. As I looked around, I saw something in them that I had no eagerness to resemble. Hannah's best friend's mother was there as well, drinking and smoking pot along with the others.

My parents were upset to learn of my experimentation with pot. To make matters worse, they knew I had lost my virginity — with two girls.

"Your conduct reflects on us," my father said as the three of us sat awkwardly in the living room.

"I only used pot once," I said. "It's not something I plan to continue doing."

"Is that all you have to say?" my father said. His arms were crossed, and his face was dark with anger. "You may not realize it, but this is a big step you've taken. Besides, there's this matter of your having sex."

"Dear ..." My mom put her hand on my father's arm.

My dad turned toward her. "He knows better!"

He was right. I knew better, but I had no religious convictions of my own. I believed my personal responsibilities before God were settled by virtue of membership in a family of preachers. I had no personal commitment to God.

Because of my choices, I was restricted from participating in video production at my church, which I had been doing for months. My parents didn't budge on their position, which meant not only more confrontations with them but also continued restriction from video production at church. So by my 18th birthday, I informed the church that I was quitting permanently. Then I said goodbye to my folks and moved in with Steve, a close friend of Hannah's who lived in his parents' garage like it was his own house.

Steve and I smoked marijuana day and night. On weekends we cranked it up with beer and often hard liquor.

We were free from supervision, and I denied myself nothing. I acted on every impulse and continued fighting with anyone who crossed me. Eventually, I began experimenting with ecstasy, LSD and magic mushrooms, as well.

However, parties must be funded, so I got a job working for a tech company, running high-speed Internet wire and installing security systems. It was a great opportunity, but because I spent all my money on partying, I couldn't afford the tools I needed. So I stole them. I was very good at stealing; nearly as good as the people who were paid to prevent it. I became a felon at age 20.

Not long after my clash with the law, Steve got pinched for possession and was court-ordered to rehab. Soon, I was dating his girlfriend, Karla. I enrolled in classes at a technical college and began studying editing and filmography. It was a productive and enjoyable time. Because of my major, I was allowed to sign out school equipment and go snowboarding and paintballing, film it and receive credit toward my degree. My instructor was a middle-aged hippie who had shot videos for the Seattle band Alice in Chains. He encouraged me to toke up as often as I liked during classes and projects. I convinced myself I actually did better work when I was high.

Karla introduced me to her friends Clay and Jeremy, and the four of us became inseparable. Clay had connections for a dozen different illegal drugs and was one of his own best customers. Though all of us were in school and kept up with our studies (and occasional jobs for the income), the centerpiece of our lives and our friendship was getting high. Our evenings and weekends were full of activity, too — snowboarding, BMX bicycling and all-around adventure. We shared a bond of trust and camaraderie. Clay, in particular, was like a brother to me.

My parents sat me down one day to discuss their plans to move out of state. By this time, they had softened toward me, not because they accepted my lifestyle, but because they didn't want to push me away entirely. I was living with them again, and they had even helped me with funding for school.

"Your mother and I are going to start a church," Dad told me.

At the same time, Karla's situation at home grew critical. Her mother had a habit of striking her with closed fists. Her stepfather, who didn't like her, did nothing to prevent it. Around the time my parents announced their move, Karla's mother finally injured her seriously. While they made plans to move, my parents invited Karla to move in, under the condition that I move out. So I moved in with my friend Mick.

Meanwhile, Karla and I both got vibes about following my parents. I was no longer in school, and Karla had written her family off. There was nothing standing in our way, and we agreed that a change would be beneficial. During the month after my parents left, we made preparations to move near them.

For the next eight months, Karla and I were different people. We stopped using substances, other than an occasional beer or two. I got a job working construction and started lending a hand at my father's new church.

There was plenty to do, since we were launching a church from scratch. The first meetings took place in a house.

We were happy. The geographical relocation had done wonders for us. Then one day, Karla called me in the middle of the day. She was crying.

"Samuel," she said, her breath whistling in and out, "Clay is dead."

"What?!"

"He's *dead*."

Jeremy had just called Karla with the news. Clay had begun selling weed after we left and sold a large quantity to three oily-looking young men who then claimed Clay had ripped them off. This was their explanation for what happened the night Clay died.

After the initial buy had taken place, one of the men called Clay asking to meet so they could get more. Clay met them in a park around 10 p.m. As he was getting off his bicycle, they set on him with rocks and a butcher knife. He fought well in spite of having a caved-in skull from the first rock blow and several deep wounds from the butcher knife. Finally, the knife went directly into his spine, paralyzing him. He bled out as they took his backpack off his body and stole his shoes right off his feet.

I wept bitterly after I hung up the phone. I didn't believe for a minute that Clay had ripped these men off. In my heart, I knew the men had made up the story to justify robbing him. In the first place, Clay was found dead with an ounce of weed and $500 on his person, which his attackers had apparently missed. Ripping someone off during a drug deal is the behavior of someone who is broke, which Clay clearly was not.

But beyond that, Clay wasn't the type to steal, even if he had been strapped. He was about the most decent person I had ever met. He was the first person in his family to complete high school.

Clay's death couldn't have come at a worse time. I had just seen him a few weeks before while I was up in Washington to settle a speeding ticket. We'd sat in his trailer and talked for hours.

"Samuel, it's lonely up here since you and Karla left," he told me. He was in tears. "The whole crew is scattered. I don't have any friends here anymore. I'm scared."

I promised him I would come visit him again soon. However, his birthday came and went, and I hadn't even picked up the phone to call him. Now I was cursing myself.

Karla and I flew back to Washington the next morning after receiving the news about Clay. By this time, I had learned from Jeremy that two of the three suspects had been apprehended, but the third was still running from the police in a wooded area in Northwest Washington. I intended to get to the murderer first and kill him, but the police caught up with him while we were still in the air. We attended Clay's funeral three days later.

I cried for days. Clay had been the best friend I'd ever had. His violent death threw me into such turmoil that when I found the partial baggie of weed in my room back home, I didn't even pause. I went to the nearest convenience store, bought a pack of rolling papers and fired it up. A week later, an old friend mentioned that he had a line on magic mushrooms, and I didn't think twice.

I spent the next four hours on the edge of insanity. During one of the hallucinations, I was staring into the bathroom mirror when Clay walked in.

"What's up?" he said. It was his normal greeting.

"You're dead," I told him.

"I know. But you'll be fine without me."

Afterward, I spent the next hour in the fetal position, thinking I was seconds away from death. I found some paper and a pen and started writing letters to my family, telling them that I loved them and was sorry for letting them down.

I woke up the next morning covered in letters.

❧❧❧

Karla and I moved back to Washington a month later. Without much discussion, we resumed smoking pot and drinking regularly. Maybe we felt justified by what had happened to Clay. I just wanted to stop feeling.

I quickly landed a job working 80 hours a week. It was just what I wanted. I could work myself into a lather every day, come home and get plowed, go to sleep and do it all over again the next day. I was too tired to notice how much I still hurt. Underneath the fatigue and the intoxication, I knew I was signing up for disaster, especially when I added cocaine into the mix. Karla had been using it for some time when I finally gave in and tried it. After a few months, I began to love the marvelous energy it gave me.

I was hardly aware how much my outlook had changed and how dependent I was on coke. Forgotten was the clean bill of health I had sought months before, the new life I had enjoyed for a time. All I had were the basics: girlfriend, work and whatever comforts could be bought with cash. Everything else was out the window.

A few months later, I discovered that Karla had started flirting with one of my friends, a seedy fellow whose own mother wouldn't allow him in her house. I snapped and ordered Karla to leave immediately. I was so angry that I refused to let her take any of her things with her.

"I paid for these things!" I told her bitingly. "You just use them. Now get out."

After Karla was gone, cocaine became my replacement woman. I used every day, at work and at home. I was walking a slippery road. Before long, no one wanted to be around me because of my drug addiction and outbursts of rage. I was consistently too high to leave my house, so I stopped going to work.

Each morning, I got up feeling worse. I was unbearably lonely, even after Jack moved in to keep me company. Finally, I woke up and decided I was going to say goodbye. I went into the living room, snorted a huge pile of cocaine and walked into the garage. I intended to hang myself, so I climbed up onto the pool table and hung a noose from the rafters. As I placed it around my neck, I thought I should say some last words. If they were my last words, they had to be good. As I stood there, on the brink of suicide, the cocaine kicked in. *I don't want to die,* I thought. *I just want to get high.* So I went back into the living room for another line.

This happened three days in a row: up from my bed ready to die, a huge line of coke, my "green mile" into the garage and my head in the noose. Then the coke would kick in as I was trying to find my last words.

I decided I would use drugs until I died, or until I didn't want to die anymore. I started gobbling ecstasy like candy. I descended into a savage state in which I never left my house and have no recollection of showering or taking meals. For a while, I was unaware of what month it was. I was using 5 to 7 grams of coke each night and huge quantities of ecstasy, pot, LSD and mushrooms to come down. I went to bed high and woke up high.

At some point, I made the inevitable discovery: I was out of money. I hadn't worked in months. My solution was to start selling drugs. My house was already a known party center, and before long I had scores of paying customers. So the party went on, although I wasn't enjoying it much. The pain I was burying under a mountain of drugs came out in bursts of violent rage. I routinely fought with anyone I thought deserved a beating. I soon realized that I could increase my sales by going mobile. Soon, I was driving all over Northwest Washington doing deals. I sold (and used) everything that was available. Nothing was off limits.

I had been dealing with a guy named Kye, who was in his mid-20s and, as I was to find out, was getting his weed from some Canadian dealers. They would come down across the border with a large quantity, give it to Kye on advance, take the cash he had made selling the last batch (minus the profits) and go back up to Canada.

One of the weaknesses of people who both use and sell drugs is that they have to keep doing transactions to keep their own drug treadmill going. The deals are even more important because drug habits have a way of increasing and absorbing all the incoming funds. This is what was happening to me. My solution, however, was to do more deals.

I met up with a grubby stranger named Jess one night who asked me to arrange a deal for some acquaintances of his to buy several pounds of weed. I agreed, even though I sensed something was wrong. I called Kye and told him I had some buyers, but I made it clear that the deal would be between him and Jess. I was just the go-between. Kye agreed to meet with us. Jack came along for security. Jess had insisted on driving us in his car, so we piled in and left.

"Listen, buddy," I told Jess. "This is your deal. I have kind of a bad feeling about this. You better be sure this is legit. If it's not, I'm not responsible. I'm just taking you to this guy I know."

"Don't worry, just tell me where we're going," he answered tightly.

I knew something was wrong, but all I could think

about was getting $800 just for making some introductions. So we drove on.

We pulled into the park where we had agreed to meet. Kye got out of his car, came over and climbed in with us. I handed the cash over to him, and he handed me a bulging grocery store bag that had been stapled shut. Kye got back into his car, and we drove away. I have no idea why we didn't check the bag.

After we'd driven most of the way back to my place, I couldn't stand it anymore.

"We'd better check this out," I said to Jess. "Just to be sure." I opened the bag and discovered 5 pounds of trimmings inside it. Trimmings are stems and leaves — the stuff that gets cut off because no one wants to buy it. I was sunk.

Jess was furious. Instead of turning onto my road, he continued straight toward his place. All I could think about was the fact that I was soon going to be discussing this with several very angry, disreputable people, probably armed.

"Listen, man," I said, my voice halfway to a shout, "I told you this was your deal. This is b******t! You need to turn this car around."

"You just keep quiet," he said in a low, threatening voice. "We're going to go work this out."

We came screeching into his driveway 10 minutes later. As Jack and I got out of the car, Jess grabbed each of us by a sleeve and dragged us into the house. Once inside, he pushed us both down on the couch.

"You'd better get this straightened out — *now*!" Jess said. "My guys are hardnosed business associates. They're not going to eat this. If you don't fix this, you guys are both dead!"

"Listen, I didn't do this," I insisted. "I got screwed over along with you. I'll fix it! I'll find them!" I promised, although I didn't have the first clue how. All I could think about was what I was going to do when I caught up with Kye.

"You think I'm just going to let you walk out the door?" Jess said.

"What am I going to do?" I asked. "You know where I live. I can't fix this sitting on your couch."

So he let us go.

A week later, while I was still trying to track Kye down, I was across the street at a neighbor's house when someone banged on the door. My neighbor walked up and looked through the peephole.

"It's those guys that got ripped off!" he said. "They've come to collect. Run out the back door!"

"No," I said. "They know where I live. Just stay inside, no matter what."

I walked to the door, opened it and stepped out into the driveway. I was surrounded by 10 men standing in a half circle. Most of them had chains or clubs. Two were clutching leashes with snarling dogs on the ends of them.

"Are you ready to die, motherf*****?" asked a burly man on my left. He had a length of chain coiled around his fist.

I knew if I showed my fear, the beating would commence quickly.

"Don't do me any favors," I said.

The burly man rattled the chain. "I don't think you're getting it. We're about to break every bone in your body. You're going to be cold and stiff when this is over."

I don't know where I found the nerve, but I looked him straight in the eye. "This isn't my doing," I said. "But I'm trying to clean it up. Now either start swinging or get out of my way so I can find the guy who ripped you off."

The guy just looked at me, amazed. Then I started walking down the driveway without looking back. They let me pass, and I crossed the street and went into my house. I sat down on the couch, shaking like a leaf. I had come very close to dying.

I tracked Kye and his friends down through a sister of a friend who was dating one of them. They were dug in at a house where there were known to be gun-wielding lunatics at all hours. Everyone I spoke to told me the same thing: "You can't break in there. People have gotten shot trying."

In that moment, all my pain and rage welled up as if on cue, with no inhibitions to check them. I was hopped up on coke to the point where someone could have severed one of my limbs and I wouldn't have felt a thing. Worst of all, I had a problem with these men that wasn't going away. If I couldn't get in, they weren't getting out. I had to act.

I decided I was going to burn the house down around

them. Surely the idea was insane, but the more I thought about it, the more my rage crackled inside me. I was going to do it. I would go around the whole house pouring gasoline on the siding. The flames would completely engulf the building, and they would be unable to escape. They would pay the ultimate penalty.

I purchased two 5-gallon containers and filled them with gas. It was a Friday, and I decided that Monday would be the day. Knowing instinctively that I might well be dead or in jail after I had carried out my plans, I gave myself a margin of two days, give or take. I intended to party like there was no tomorrow — for, indeed, there might not be.

That day, I did the usual and snorted several grams of cocaine. I finished up in the wee hours and, also as usual, took a handful of ecstasy tablets and a baggie full of mushrooms. I would wake up in the morning higher than a kite.

ન્જન્જન્જ

The first thing I was aware of the next morning was the sense that everything was wrong. In the first place, it seemed way too early for me to be waking up. The sun was just coming up over the horizon. More bizarre still was the fact that I was dead sober. It was impossible, but I didn't feel the least bit fuzzy. Everything felt straight and sharp. My mind felt clearer than it had been for more than a year. Suddenly, I saw the whole previous year with frightening clarity. My decision to move back to Washington, my swift transition from clean, sober, employed and responsible to what I was now — jobless, criminal, drug-addicted and nearing death. I thought, *I did this to myself, every bit of it.*

I opened the door of my bedroom and looked out. There were people passed out on the floor in the hallway and, beyond them, in the living room.

I had stepped over these people a hundred times, but now seeing them there, they were like proof of my complete failure, as were the empty beer and whiskey bottles strewn all around.

I felt a voice inside speaking so softly that there were no words, only impressions.

This is what you've done to yourself, the voice seemed to say. *And now you're about to kill some people in a house fire. Do you really want to do this? There will be no coming back from it. Your life will be changed forever.*

All the while, my mind felt amazingly clear. The implications of the decision before me were razor sharp. I was completely calm. My feelings of anger and loneliness, the pain of Karla's betrayal — all of it had been lifted away without explanation. I looked out again into my living room at the sprawled bodies on the floor. Such a waste. This was what I was, too, save for this impossible clarity that had come to me as the sun's warm rays shone over the hills in the distance.

This, I thought, had to be the hand of God.

Without thinking, I reached into my front pocket,

pulled out my phone and dialed my father. He answered after two rings.

"How are you doing, son?" he said.

"Dad," I said into the phone, "I need to come home."

෴෴෴

There were many difficult months and years ahead. The process of getting clean and sober wasn't a straight line, nor was my journey into maturity.

One stint in rehab and a broken marriage later (I was married and divorced in just a few years), I was revisited by the same clarity that had hit me in my living room a day before I was going to torch a houseful of people. This time, I felt the same warm force drawing me back to church and, more importantly, toward God. I had taken steps (mainly stopping my use of drugs), but now I understood how much further there was to go. I saw my faults with utter clarity and longed for what lay ahead — which God was making available to me the same way he had before.

I still struggle occasionally with my feelings toward other races, but I understand now that the people who lashed out and bullied me were just hurting people themselves. They were trying to cover their own pain, insecurities and shame.

I approached God for my own reasons. For a time, I ignored the expectations and criticism of others. I wanted whatever relationship I had with God to be real, not some attempt to please the people in my life, no matter how well meaning they might be.

I began reading the Bible and communicating daily with God. As I practiced these disciplines and enjoyed the fellowship of my friends at Champion Life Church, I became a different person. Periodically, I looked at my life and realized that it was steadily getting better. My church became a second home. It was there, in the foyer of my church, as I was arriving one afternoon, late and nearly running to make the service, that I heard a familiar voice inside speak three words: *Look behind you.*

I did, and the only person there in that whole stretch of the building was an attractive brunette woman standing quietly next to the windows. She looked up at me when I stopped.

"Hi," I said.

"Hi," she said back.

I had just met my wife.

‏‍‎‏ ‏‍‎‏ ‏‍‎‏

As I look back on my life, I see the hand of God everywhere. When I was still in diapers, I wandered into my grandparents' barn and into one of the pens, where a cow was nursing her calf. The mother responded in defense of her calf and tried to grind me into the floor with her head. Then she began throwing me against the walls of the pen, again with her head. By the time my father arrived, I was turning blue from lack of breath. He carried me out of the barn, yelling for help as he ran. My mother arrived on the scene, took me from my father's arms and started running down the road toward my grandparents' house.

My grandfather had a reputation as a prayer warrior and a keen instinct as well. He was sitting in his chair as my mother burst through the door. When she got within a few feet of him, she threw me into his arms.

"He's not breathing!" my mom screamed, but Grandpa was already praying. Within a few moments, my complexion changed from dark blue-back to white. My breathing was perfectly normal.

Another time, my family was driving home one evening when I was 4. I was riding in the backseat with my sister and managed to polish off an entire bottle of Children's Tylenol, thinking they were candy. My mother felt a prodding in her spirit as she looked back and saw me sleeping soundly in the backseat. Something told her to rummage through the bags in the back. She promptly found the empty Tylenol bottle, and my father drove straight to a fire station, where I have hazy memories of my grandfather carrying me around a fire truck as I vomited into a coffee can. They had given me sulphur to induce vomiting.

Perhaps the greatest evidence of God's loving-kindness is the fact that I emerged sane and whole from so many near-death experiences — literally from the cusp of the grave. In so many cases, I *knew the risks* and yet proceeded on. God's mercy astounds me to this day.

My father tells parts of my story often while addressing his congregation, though there are many details he still hasn't heard. Many pastors wouldn't dare disclose such things about their sons, and many congregations wouldn't trust a pastor who did. The culture at his church, however, is built upon a recognition that we are all flawed and struggle with sin. The clincher is that God knows it, too, and understands. The church is meant to be an infirmary, not a courthouse. My father openly discusses my season in flight from God without shame. As for me, I have no regrets. I consider every minute of my past as part of God's overall redemptive plan for my life.

This conviction crystallized for me one evening after a long midweek service I attended at his church. My father had been particularly emotional this night, and he had unabashedly told of some of my hardest experiences and the fear he had felt while I was going through them. Afterward, as he always does, he brought my story to the present, lest anyone in the pews might think I am still out there courting death.

"My son is here tonight, clean and sober for seven years. He's right here in the front row, with his wife and baby daughter." I waved and rose halfway, clutching Emily Rose in one arm. There was applause, but I talked to God silently. *That's for you, Lord. You did this.*

Later, as I was socializing in the foyer, a middle-aged woman came up to me shyly. She looked as though she had been weeping.

"Excuse me, are you Samuel? The pastor's son?"

"Yes, I am!"

"I just want to thank you. When your father shared your story tonight, I almost thought he was talking about my son for a moment. You see, my David has been through the same things you went through. Only he's still out there. He's tried to kill himself twice. He's been through rehabs and everything, but he can't seem to stay away from the drugs. I wrote him off two years ago. I thought it was best for the family. But I'm going to call him when I get home tonight."

Now the woman began weeping with great intensity, her whole body shaking. "I still love him, you see," she said through her tears. "And you and that father of yours have given me hope that David can make it out of this yet. God bless you!" And she put her hands up to my face.

I couldn't speak. I was blown away. In that moment, I realized how powerfully God can use our human failures, if only we will get around to trusting him and walking with him. At the same time, I saw how far God had brought me — right from the cusp of the grave.

JOURNEY OUT OF PAIN
The Story of Gwen
Written by Sharon Kirk Clifton

The sun streamed in through the sliding glass doors, belying the tempest I was going through in the middle of the living room floor.

"Why are you putting me through this hell?" My cry bounced off the ceiling. "I can't tolerate it any longer! It has to stop!"

I wrapped my arms around myself and rocked back and forth, like a forsaken child. Where was Sean? I needed him to hold me tight. Why wasn't he here? Stupid question. He was at the showroom where he belonged. I was supposed to be working here at home, but I couldn't. Not with the timpani section pounding inside my head.

"You promised me. You said you'd give me wisdom," I screamed again. "Where is my wisdom? You said I wouldn't have to go through anything too great for me to handle. Well, I can't handle THIS!"

I slumped forward, feeling dead inside. I'd depleted all my resources.

I had come to the end of myself.

≈≈≈

Mine is no rags-to-riches story. Money was always plentiful — growing up, anyway. My grandparents, professional entertainers, were well-fixed financially. Grandma Maureen was a professional dancer by age 16, performing in nightclubs with her sister Laura. That's how Grandma met Grandpa Rich. He was a musician. Played a mean saxophone. Any kind of horn, really. They eloped when she was 16 and he was 20. Grandpa played with the Freddy Martin band and even did a stint with the Glenn Miller Orchestra. My grandparents loved the money — making it and spending it.

Mom grew up in that world, so it was natural that she became a dancer, and a good one at that. Since she had a gift for teaching, she ran a thriving tap and jazz dance studio, where she pushed her students, including my older brother, Paul, and me, to shine on the stage. Several of her tutees went on to make names for themselves, as well.

My happiest childhood memories revolve around that dance studio. Though Mom drove us especially hard when we were getting ready for a recital, I loved it, loved everything about it — the dancing, the costumes, the makeup, the accolades, the sparkle, Mom's approval after the curtain call — the whole package. Life at the studio was fun, like Never-Never Land.

Home was another story. Mom left Ray, my biological father, when I was very young. I was 6 months old when they divorced. A succession of stepfathers followed.

Harry was stepdad number one, husband number two. I was a year old when he married Mom and 5 when my half-brother, Troy, was born. For the nine years they were married, we lived on an emotional rollercoaster.

Harry drank heavily. When he was sober, life was fun. He knew how to be kind, sometimes even jovial. However, he had a temper, and when he drank, terror reigned. We all cowered before his wrath. He was an angry drunk. Every night at dinner, we had stomachaches, fearing what might happen. We sat at the dinner table afraid to utter a word, keeping our eyes averted as we forked our food around on our plates, only occasionally lifting a bite to our mouths. He was a ticking bomb, and we didn't know how much time remained before the explosion. Images of his violent assaults on Mom — his full-force slaps across her face, leaving behind a scarlet handprint that would morph into a bruise; his grabbing her by the hair and jerking her around to face a drunken tirade of accusations and obscenities; his throwing her into a corner, as though she were a wad of soiled laundry, and beating her, vile images all — remain branded on my memory.

At such times, I tried to protect Troy from witnessing the full impact of his father's actions. With him in tow, I'd run away from the violence. Holding hands, we'd hunker down in my closet, and I'd pray.

"God, help us. Please stop Harry. Please, God. Oh, Jesus, make him stop!"

I knew to pray because when I visited my birth father, my stepmother, Diane, a Christian, told me about Jesus. I was 7 when she showed me a little book that had no words, only colors. The first page was black.

"This represents our sin," she said. "Sin is the things we do that break God's heart. Everyone sins."

Then she turned to a red page. "Because God loves us so much, he sent his only Son, Jesus, to die in our place, to pay the price for the bad things we do."

The next page was pure white.

"When we tell Jesus we're sorry for our sins and that we want to follow him, to live the way he wants us to, he takes away our sin. Our hearts are clean then. White as lamb's wool."

After that came the gold page, my favorite. She explained that when people who love Jesus die, they go to be with him in heaven.

"The Bible says the streets of heaven are paved with pure gold. Imagine that!"

I did.

The cover of the Wordless Book was a brilliant grass green. "For growth," she said. "Once someone becomes a Christian, she wants to grow in her faith. She does that by talking to him — that's called prayer — and letting him talk to her. He does that through the Bible." That day, I knelt beside her sofa and told Jesus I wanted to follow him.

Diane's mom gave me a Bible of my own, so I read it and prayed every night.

Harry's rages prompted me to pray, also. A lot.

☙☙☙

Then one October night in 1976, everything changed.

I had spent most of my younger life in Long Beach,

California, but when I was 10, we moved to Yucca Valley. Mom claimed she wanted to retire from teaching dance. She also said the change would take away some of Harry's stress.

"Life in the desert will be calmer." She thought he might lighten up on the drinking and violence if we lived in a more relaxed environment.

Her retirement from teaching didn't last long. Harry was struggling to make money. Mom loved activity and the money she could earn by teaching, so she opened another studio. Turned out there was a demand for good dance instructors, and her business soon thrived, as it always had.

Moving to the desert did nothing to alleviate Harry's drinking problem. One night, he and Mom left Paul, Troy and me with a babysitter while they and my grandparents attended a Jaycee gala in town. In the middle of the night, someone shook me awake. The babysitter, an older woman, said my family had come to take us home. I wondered why the lights were off. It was dark, and we could barely make our way through the house. Mom was standing like a dark shadow near the door. We got into Grandpa Rich's car, and he drove us to his house, not ours.

In the house, with the lights on, I saw Mom. She wore the full-length white mink coat I'd seen her in earlier.

Except it was no longer white. It was covered in blood, and blood streamed down my mother's face from a gash on her forehead.

"Mom! What happened?"

I think I cried. Surely I did. *So much blood,* I thought. *Will you live, Mom? Or are you going to die?* I wished I could hide Troy from the sight. After all, he was only 5. If I didn't protect him, who would? Not Mom. She couldn't even save herself from Harry's fury.

I later learned what had ignited his rage that night. Something had happened at the Jaycee affair to incite his jealousy. When he got Mom to the car, he locked the doors so she couldn't escape and beat her. Mercilessly. One blow cracked her on the forehead with such force that it broke the skin and severed a vein. His brutality also left her with a couple cracked ribs. The next morning, she went to the ER. Her forehead required stitches, and she ended up staying one night in the hospital.

After nine years of marriage, my mother divorced Harry. We had survived that ugly chapter of our lives.

శ్రీ శ్రీ శ్రీ

Though violence walked out the door with Harry, instability and insecurity stayed behind.

Less than a year later, Mom remarried. Enter stepfather number two, Donald. He was a strict disciplinarian. He held us to a high standard and invoked a regimen of expectations.

I had a list of chores to do before school. Mom loved to cook, and she prepared huge dinners that dirtied a lot of dishes. After dinner, we'd load the dishwasher and start it. It was my job each morning to unload it and put away the dishes.

Though Donald never laid a hand on Mom, they argued a lot. If it was a big fight, we left.

"Pack your things," Mom would say. "We're moving out." From November 1977 to August 1984, we moved more than 40 times. We'd go from the spaciousness of Donald's home into cramped rental housing. It was hardly worth unpacking, because we knew that as soon as things calmed down, we'd be back with Donald. When we were all back together, we kids tried to keep peace in the home and keep down the fighting so Mom wouldn't get angry again and move us out.

It was never Donald's idea for us to leave. That was wholly Mom. Donald provided us with a stable home. A couple times, Paul got sick of moving.

"I'm staying here with Donald," he announced. I wished I could do the same, but I had to go with Mom.

Donald was the closest thing to a father figure I had. I called him a brainiac because he knew so much about so many things. He pushed all three of us to achieve in school, too. He treated me as though I were his daughter, his real blood daughter. And he encouraged me in my dancing.

I was 11 years old when we held a recital I'll never forget. I danced a routine to the song "Let Me Entertain You" wearing a pink sequined costume, fishnet tights, a pink feather boa and my tap shoes. After the show, Donald met me with a broad smile on his face.

"You looked so beautiful out there," he said. "And I am so proud of you."

Around the time I was 15, Mom began divorce proceedings against Donald. That made me so sad. I went to his office and asked why Mom was divorcing him.

"Your mom can't settle for a silver lining. She wants a gold one." I took that to mean she wanted a perfect marriage and a perfect life. Even as a teenager, I knew neither existed.

As if to prove the point, Mom became involved with two other men after Donald. She was married to one briefly.

ॐॐॐ

I discovered Sean when I was in high school. We were riding on the school bus. I was a cheerleader, and he was a basketball player. He was super smart and smokin' hot. He had the most amazing eyes, too. As I got to know him, I learned that he had a sweet spirit to complement his good looks — unlike most of the men Mom had brought into our lives. He was the first boy I dated. He won my heart.

When I was 17, two big events happened. I graduated high school, and I moved in with Sean. No longer did I have to contend with the assorted stepfathers.

Our happiness would have been complete, except that I worried about Troy. I hated leaving him behind. I also believed in my heart that living with Sean outside of marriage did not please God, but I had watched Mom cycle through several husbands, and I didn't want that kind of life. All the time we dated, we talked about getting married. It was something we intended to do at some point.

Three years later, in 1987, when I was 20, we married. At last, I had stability and security in my life. I also had a great job working for a company that sold upscale RV lots, going for 30 to 100 grand — and there were 1,300 of them to sell. I loved my work. I was made for it, and I did it well. From the time I walked in the door in the morning until I took off the name badge in the evening, I ran at full tilt, giving my all to every detail. Because I was good at what I did, the company piled on more and more responsibility. I did marketing and sales and secretarial duties. I also was the assistant to the director of marketing. I didn't mind. I reveled in the challenge.

Until it broke me.

෴

I was 23 when I suffered my first panic attack on January 9, 1990. At first I didn't recognize it for what it was. I thought I was losing my mind. They recurred, often in the middle of the night, crippling me, paralyzing me with fear. The first one jerked me awake. I shot straight up in bed with an adrenaline rush, heart beating super fast. It scared me so badly, I couldn't even think straight, and I couldn't shake it for three or four hours. It was horrible.

I woke Sean, but he had no idea what to do, of course,

so he went back to sleep. I don't blame him. If he'd thought there was something he could do to alleviate my anxiety, he'd have done it in a heartbeat. He didn't know how to comfort me or help me figure out how to cope with what I was feeling. If only he had taken me in his arms and held me — that would have helped.

The attacks continued night after terrifying night. The mere *fear* of having one would precipitate another. Never again did I try to wake Sean. I went, instead, to Grandma Maureen's. She had become my dearest friend. We would sleep in the guest room, or she'd just hold me until the attack passed. After a couple middle-of-the-night visits, I often stayed with her, anticipating the night terror. Being with her was the only thing that helped my torment.

Some people think such attacks are the result of stress or that stopping them is as simple as reasoning them away. A little self-talk will do the trick. *Okay. This is ridiculous. I have absolutely no reason to feel this way. I have a good life, a loving husband, a supportive family, a great job. Stop it. Just stop it!* I tried that. It didn't work.

Three months in, Grandma took me to see a medical doctor.

"You're having panic attacks," he said. Until that moment, I had no name for what was going on other than *crazy.* He prescribed a medicine that did nothing to alleviate the attacks, but did make me sleepy.

Then I went to a Christian psychologist who tried to help. I memorized a Bible verse and recited it over and over in the middle of the night, using it as a prayer for healing. Even that didn't help. I listened to subliminal tapes. Still no relief. Sometimes I would get up and run around and around the block until I was exhausted. On a couple occasions, I lay down on the desert in the dark and just cried. Then I went home and to bed. I finally drifted off to sleep, only to be jerked awake by another panic attack.

My body blocked sleep because that's when the onslaught came. I couldn't let down my guard. Then, in my sleep-deprived state, I had to drag myself into work the next day. Though the people I worked for were very kind, granting me some time off, I couldn't abuse that grace.

As the attacks continued, my mind turned to thoughts of suicide. It seemed the only way out of that hell.

One day I was driving down Bob Hope Drive when it occurred to me that it would be so easy to ram my car into a telephone pole. If I were going fast enough, surely I would die. No more panic attacks! I'd finally be free of them. I chose a pole and aimed the car straight at it. Suddenly some thoughts rushed to center stage of my brain.

This will destroy Sean.

And Mom.

And Grandma Maureen.

And my brothers.

Will I go to heaven? If one kills herself, can she make it to heaven? Can she be with Jesus and walk those golden streets Diane spoke of?

With mere seconds to spare, I swerved away from the pole.

The attacks continued. In desperation, Sean, who was not a follower of Jesus at the time, went to the church where we were married and begged for someone to come help me. It was a Sunday.

I went to that evening's service, meeting first with a man on the pastoral staff who had himself endured panic attacks.

At the end of the service, the pastor asked if anyone needed prayer. I prayed and asked God to help me. Thus began my journey out of panic.

I finally went to see a psychiatrist who prescribed a medication that worked. I was on it for eight months, just long enough to break the cycle of anxiety. I believe that God can give a spontaneous healing, but I also believe he often uses medicines and other means to heal. I needed the medicine.

❧❧❧

I called Grandma Maureen soon after Grandpa Rich passed away.

"Grandma, sit down. I have wonderful news. You're such a great grandma, and now you're going to be a great-grandma."

Though I couldn't see her, I could imagine her face. She had the most amazing smile I've ever seen. It would begin slowly and spread across her beautiful face, engulfing every part. Her eyes would twinkle and her nose wrinkle.

"I am?" She drew out the *am* the way she said, "Gin," when she won a game. "That's grand!" I could tell from the playfulness in her voice that the news lifted the burden of grief from her shoulders. I think she must have sat up straighter, too.

Shelli was born March 13, 1992. When Shelli was a year old, Grandma came to live with us. It made so much sense. Grandpa was gone, she was rattling around a big house she was renting and her cash resources were dwindling.

We developed a comfortable routine. Grandma moved into the guest room and went to bed around 7 p.m. She was up at 5 a.m., so we had all the privacy we needed.

Sean is a gifted artist. Business was growing, so while he worked at the showroom and in his studio, I handled the tech end of the business from our home office. Having Grandma in our home freed me up considerably to do what I needed to.

We had the greatest little life, eating breakfast together, getting Shelli dressed and planning our day. I would scoot around the corner from the kitchen to my office to work, while Grandma played with the baby for three or four hours. Then we'd go grocery shopping, and Grandma would cook dinner.

What a cook my classy grandma was! She and Grandpa had owned a couple restaurants in their day, so she knew her way around a kitchen. I can still taste her tuna noodle casserole and her Swiss steak with mashed potatoes and gravy. We always had fish at least one night a week.

"I just cook plain style," she'd say. "Your momma, now she's the gourmet cook."

After dinner, I did all the cleanup. Donald, stepfather number two, had taught me well how to load and unload a dishwasher.

The four years Grandma lived with us were some of the best of my life. When she died in her sleep of a brain tumor, I was devastated. We had always been very close. She was my rock when our family endured the Harry years, my counselor through the Donald years and beyond and my dearest friend through my years as a young wife and mother.

Her passing plunged me into a profound grief that led to a crisis point in my life.

❧❧❧

It had been three months since Grandma Maureen had gone home to heaven, but I grieved her passing as if it were yesterday. When she died, I lost my rudder. Yes, I had a husband, but he wasn't who I turned to for emotional support.

I had a hard time letting her go. It was the little things. Something would happen, and I'd think, *I need to call Grandma and tell her about that,* or I'd see someone who looked like her and stop myself just before calling out her name. Shelli would bring home a craft she'd made or a picture she'd colored.

"It's so pretty. You must show that to …" I'd catch myself just in time.

"To who, Momma?"

"To your daddy, sweetheart. When he gets home."

I lived under a steel-gray cloud of sorrow. I wept much of the time. I came to realize that my grief wasn't solely for my grandmother. It was for me, also. Yes, I knew Jesus. Yes, I'd told him I wanted to live for him. But I was a poor follower. Not one Jesus would brag about.

Sean and I were good friends with three other couples. All of us were at a comfortable level financially, so we could afford to travel and party together. During that time, I became addicted to cigarettes and alcohol. It was fun. We had boats and RVs and jet skis and all that kind of stuff. I would hold a brandy in one hand, take a draw on my cigarette and talk about how much I loved Jesus. My girlfriends noticed my hypocrisy, but I didn't need them to tell me what I was doing was wrong. Worst of all, I realized that if I continued like this, Shelli would follow my example.

Was I trying to bury my grief with activity? Perhaps. Was I trying to numb my brain against my sorrow? Maybe.

I also felt guilt over my resentment of my birth father, Ray. Not long after Grandma passed, Ray divorced Diane, his wife of 30 years. I considered her a good friend — after all, she was the one who told the little 7-year-old me about

Jesus — and I intended to stay close to her. That made my father angry. He began to berate me. His verbal attacks worsened after we hired him to work in our showroom. My resentment against him grew. I came to dread every contact I had with him, but there was no way to avoid him. The nature of his position meant I had to call him often or go in to see him. He took those opportunities to verbally and emotionally attack me. Eventually, we had to let him go. Though the dismissal was justified, I felt guilty that my resentment remained.

All of those elements were at play when, on a crisp September morning in 1997, I called Mom. We were talking when her husband, a Christian, interrupted.

"Would you please tell Gwen that the Lord spoke to my spirit today? She needs to read Romans 12:1 and 2. I don't know why. I'm just the messenger."

I stood at the bar that separated my kitchen from the dining area and flipped to those verses in my Bible. "I appeal to you therefore, brothers, by the mercies of God, to present your bodies as a living sacrifice, holy and acceptable to God, which is your spiritual worship. Do not be conformed to this world, but be transformed by the renewal of your mind, that by testing you may discern what is the will of God, what is good and acceptable and perfect" (ESV).

My stepdad was right. Those verses were what I needed to read. They were the message that prompted me to finally turn to the only one who could truly help.

"Lord, I need more of you. I know you. I follow you.

Sometimes. But this isn't working. I cannot function like this, sobbing all the time, living a half-in Christian life. I need *more* of you! Take all of me, Lord. Take all I have, if that's needed for me to be an all-in believer. Half-in isn't good enough."

It occurred to me that I could lose all my friends, once I stopped partying. I could even lose Sean because he might not like the changes I made.

"Take it all, Lord, if that is required."

At last I was all in.

ৡৡৡ

In the spring of 2002, a group of friends asked me to lead a home Bible study on end-time prophecy. I struggled with that because I thought I had no business leading a Bible study. Doubts flooded my mind.

Who do you think you are, teaching this thing?

Your explanations aren't clear enough.

You said that wrong.

You can't do this. Why try?

Horrible, self-defeating thoughts!

A few months later, in July, I was leading the study. We were reading Isaiah 61 when I suddenly got an excruciating headache. I had never experienced a headache before, so this one knocked me flat. It was so intense, it made me nauseous. Pain medication didn't touch it. Nor could I sleep it off. I tried massage, aroma therapy, listening to relaxation tapes — nothing worked. I saw a neurologist who said I was healthy. The chiropractor couldn't help me, either. The pain would wax and wane, but it never went away, not for two years! I saw doctors who ordered various tests and blood work, but they could find no physical cause for my pain.

When it seemed my case was hopeless, at least from a human standpoint, one of my Christian friends suggested I consider acupuncture. I'd tried everything else; I figured I may as well try that.

The acupuncture practice was housed in a very clean, professional-looking building. It looked pretty much like any other medical facility, except for the yin and yang symbols that were a part of the décor. I went through the procedure, but felt very uncomfortable. And it didn't help ease the pain at all.

Through it all, my faith in God remained strong. I accept that sometimes he allows bad things to come into the lives of his children, but I believe they're never random. I believe they serve to make us more like the God we love. I started to suspect that the cause of my pain was spiritual, and that's why the headaches couldn't be eased even with four powerful pain meds, muscle relaxants or morphine.

I met with my pastor, and he agreed that spiritual torment could cause physical pain.

I contacted Dee, a woman who led Bible studies at church and also a ministry to help people get free from the influence of addictions or, strange as it might sound, demonic attacks. Could she help me break free of this bondage of pain? I prayed so. Dee agreed to meet with and mentor me.

Some people have headaches. Plural. I didn't. I had one horrible, unrelenting headache that lasted more than two years.

That brought me to the point where I sat crumpled in the middle of my living room floor, crying out to God for answers.

"Why are you putting me through this hell? I can't tolerate it any longer! It has to stop!" I couldn't understand. I had given my all to Christ. I was his little girl, his child. I had surrendered everything to him. Yet the pain continued like a battering ram inside my head, banging, banging, banging against my skull, interfering with every thought, every dream, every tender moment. I could sympathize with Job, a man in the Bible who endured a lot of suffering.

Dee and I met over a long period of time, and she also concluded there was a deep spiritual struggle causing my pain. We prayed, we worshipped, she counseled and we prayed some more.

Dee didn't simply pray. She fasted, eating nothing for one to three days before we met.

Then she asked God, "Where do I begin?"

She started naming my troubles, my personal demons.

"Which demon leaves first?"

She said the Lord had told her the spirit of pain would be the first to go. She ordered that spirit to leave in the name of Jesus. It took a number of weeks for the headache to end. Perhaps healing had to take place. But the headache did finally cease.

Other spirits left, also.

Unforgiveness.

Hatred.

Murder.

I pictured them like a little gang. When one left, they all left.

I felt God was trying to tell me that, while all of those things played their role in my enslavement to pain, the one I call the *gatekeeper*, the one that opened the door to torment, was unforgiveness. When Jesus gave his model prayer, showing his disciples how they should approach God as our father, he said, "Forgive us our trespasses as we forgive those who trespass against us." I was willing, eager, to have God forgive my sins, but woe to those who sinned against me! I believe the prayer makes it very clear that we will be forgiven *to the degree we forgive others.* That revelation was major to me. My pain and my unforgiveness were linked. Two cancers feeding off of one another. I had to forgive my biological father and my stepfather. With the Lord's help, I did.

At long last, I am at liberty to live in the freedom Jesus gives, free of physical or spiritual agony.

೪೪೪

Once the pain was gone, I could focus on other things. I felt like I was entering a different season of my life. I felt that God wanted me to step down from teaching the home Bible study and give my attention to our growing art business.

My friendship with Dee continued to grow. When she invited me to go with her to a service at Champion Life Church, I accepted.

I loved it. Such energy filled the auditorium. God was involved in the lives of the people there. But I had no plan to return. I also loved the church I attended at the time. I knew all the people. It felt like home. But when I went to that church the next Sunday, I felt the Lord was telling me, *You're not supposed to be here any longer.*

As I walked to my car after the service, it was like I heard a whisper: *This is the last time you'll go to your car from this church.* And it was. I had nothing against the church or anyone in it. I just felt my time to move on had come.

I dove into Champion Life headfirst and quickly became involved in helping with the services. I'm a tech person. Is it a gift from God? I don't know, but all things tech come naturally to me.

Soon I was helping with anything technical related to the worship services and other special events. Lighting effects, sound, projection — even the stage fog machines. (Our church services are more like rock concerts.) I loved it!

CLC had a unique program that piqued my interest when I heard it announced: Marketplace Ministry.

"Sign up to learn more about finances and how your

participation in Marketplace Ministry can help enlarge the kingdom."

That sounded great to me. I'd never heard of the concept before and wanted to learn more.

Sean still wasn't a Christ-follower. It would have made me happy for him to have gone with me, but for now, Shelli and I went together. I was okay with that until Pastor Tammy Windsor, wife of our lead pastor, Eddie, and Pastor Linda Carpenter called me on it.

"Gwen, why don't you invite Sean to come with you and Shelli?"

"He's not interested," I said.

Linda shook her head. "You can't *settle*. Don't be complacent. Cry out to Jesus on behalf of your husband. Stand firm, believing he will come to church and give his life to Christ."

Our business was expanding rapidly, and Sean was working long hours every day. He was exhausted most of the time, and it was affecting him emotionally. It made him angry, even mean, much of the time, so I was somewhat apprehensive about approaching him. But I had a mission — to captivate Sean for Christ's sake. When I heard about Marketplace Ministry, I realized that might be a way to get him to come.

"Sweetheart, they have a new program starting up at church. It's a series of classes. They'll talk about finances and how to use one's money for Christ. I plan to attend. Will you come with me?"

He looked across the table at me and smiled.

"Definitely."

What? It was supposed to be harder than that. Where was the argument, the grumble, the excuse? It was as though he'd been waiting for me to invite him.

It turned out that Sean had been listening to Dave Ramsey's radio program on Christian finances for months. He knew more about God's plan for our budget, both business and private, than I did, and he was eager to learn more.

I used to dream I would be in church one day, and when the pastor told us to turn around and greet someone, I'd feel a hand on my shoulder, turn and see Sean standing there. He'd smile and say, "Surprise!" Then, at the invitation to come forward and accept Christ as Savior and Lord, he'd do it. But that isn't the way it went down.

God used Marketplace Ministry to pull my husband through the church doors and up to the feet of Jesus.

As we attended the classes, we began applying the precepts we learned to our own business, and we multiplied our tithing.

God blessed us beyond anything we could have imagined. We gave. He gave more. We gave more. He upped the blessings.

We'd made it a rule to live below our means so we could pay cash for what was needed. In order to grow our business, though, we needed a bigger building. We set our sights on one property. To acquire it, we would need to invest nearly all the money we had. We felt God was prompting us to step out in faith and get it, so we followed his urging.

Of course, blessings don't guarantee protection from suffering or stress. This time, Sean is the one who suffered. As the business grew, so did the pressures. Sean was working 18-hour days on the new building. When he finally made it home, he was exhausted and downright mean to Shelli and me, snapping at us over the simplest things. Finally, I'd had enough, and I confronted him. My approach wasn't the most winsome.

"Sean, do you realize how you treat me and our daughter here at home? I know you're tired. You're working too many hours and not allowing yourself any time to rest. Honey, sometimes you're downright mean."

I had his attention. "I won't tolerate that. I had to live with it through assorted stepfathers, but I won't accept it in our home. Things have to change. Either go to counseling, go to church or move out." He looked at me, devoid of expression. "I'm serious." For a moment, neither of us spoke.

"Okay."

"Okay what?" I prayed he wasn't saying, *Okay, leave.*

"Okay, I'll go."

I love that man so much! He began attending church services, and once again, God brought healing.

He also continues to bless us financially. Shortly after our marriage began to heal, we felt as though God looked down on us and said, "I see you. I know you're living according to my principles. I notice how you faithfully give of your resources, your time and your talents. Now, I want to give you something special."

We were awarded a contract that would earn for us an average year's income in one project. Shortly after that, we were commissioned to create a special tribute to a former U.S. president. We could never have anticipated either of those plums, but God did.

One of the best gifts from God was seeing my baby brother, Troy, overcome his own set of life troubles. He's a gifted man of God and a valued employee of our company. We are so thankful that my mom and stepdad have decided to become followers of Jesus, as well.

Sean and I love serving God through Champion Life Church. We love the people and the fellowship, we enjoy the friendship of the ministry team. Because I'm usually busy with the tech team during services, we seldom get to sit together in a worship service, but it's enough for me to know Sean's there and faithfully involved — because he chooses to be. God continues to bless us personally and professionally as we serve him wherever and however we can.

"I waited patiently for the LORD; he inclined to me and heard my cry. He drew me up from the pit of destruction, out of the miry bog, and set my feet upon a rock, making my steps secure. He put a new song in my mouth, a song of praise to our God. Many will see and fear, and put their trust in the LORD." (Psalm 40:1-3)

NEW BEGINNINGS
The Story of Zoe and Damion
Written by Angela Welch Prusia

Dr. Krieger set down my chart. Concern swept professionalism aside, and I saw my friend, the doctor I'd seen since high school. The same gynecologist trusted by my mother for years.

Something was wrong.

"Zoe, you won't be able to have children unless you change your habits." Compassion softened Dr. Krieger's face. "Your body's monthly cycle is interrupted."

I gulped. I'd brushed aside my worries for months.

"You're starving yourself of protein and other vital nutrients," she continued. "There's no fuel to keep up your vigorous exercise regimen."

My lip quivered at the death sentence. I wanted five kids, evenly spaced in years, not long after I married my prince. According to my plan, we'd meet before my graduation from college in two years.

"Are you sure?" I wanted to ask, but knew Dr. Krieger spoke the truth. I twirled the purity ring on my ring finger, the one given to me by my father at age 15. Light glinted off the small diamonds encircling an aquamarine stone, reminding me of the night my father had taken me to dinner at an upscale restaurant. He'd looked so handsome in his suit and tie, while I felt beautiful in a black semi-formal dress.

Wait for him.

Daddy's words echoed in my head whenever I dated young men, including the wild football jock who I dated throughout high school, hoping I could rescue him by bringing him with me to youth group and summer church camp. I waited, saving my virginity as a precious gift for my future husband.

But now what?

What would I tell my prince when we finally met? Would he want a princess who couldn't have children?

"Eat a pizza." Dr. Krieger's voice broke my thoughts. "Enjoy a hamburger."

Her smile brought little comfort. The very thought of greasy food made me want to hurl.

I hadn't eaten fast food in years, choosing only low- and non-fat foods to eat. I prided myself in my meticulous calorie counting and disciplined exercise routine.

I drove home in a fog. Beside me, my mother squeezed my hand in gentle reassurance.

"You okay?"

I nodded. Dr. Krieger was just being cautious. *How could my healthy habits threaten my ability to have children?*

Back at Abilene Christian University, I discovered a note on my pillow from my roommate, Jenny.

"I love you like a sister, Zoe. Otherwise I couldn't write this. But I'm worried about how little you eat and how much you exercise."

Tears trailed down my face.

Jenny expressed the same concerns as both my mother and doctor. It was time to stop living in denial.

I wasn't hungry, but I grabbed a yogurt, anyway, and headed to the library on campus to work on my research paper. Ironically, I'd chosen the topic which now plagued me — eating disorders.

Alone, as I poured over medical articles on anorexia and bulimia, I was surprised to learn that the underlying causes of eating disorders had nothing to do with food.

Shock rooted me to the chair. Words jumped off the page, the description so perfect, I stared in a mirror.

Perfectionism.

Low self-esteem.

Feelings of unworthiness.

Desire for control.

Obsessive tendencies.

I pushed the articles aside and stared into space. Memories I'd tried to stuff for years crowded my mind, demanding my attention.

The petite girl who got teased by the mean kids because of her physical limitations. *How could they know I'd been deprived of oxygen at 6 days old, nearly dying from Sudden Infant Death Syndrome? They didn't hear my mother call out the name of Jesus until I gulped in air.*

The same girl who learned to control the pain by feigning sickness in P.E. class.

She was always the last person to be chosen for any team.

The wallflower sitting alone in her new private

Christian school dressed in the uniform she despised, refusing to make friends. If only her parents saw her misery, surely they would move back to her old neighborhood.

The awkward teenager who felt more comfortable hanging out with her brother than shopping at the mall with gossipy girls.

The driven college student with the insane class load pursuing a double major in four years.

I blinked back the fresh wave of pain. *What difference did Dr. Krieger's news mean? Who would ever want to marry someone so unworthy of love?*

Why hope for happily ever after if the beginning started like this?

ॐॐॐ

Someone dimmed the lights at our sorority meeting the following week, and excitement swept the room. The president adjourned the meeting and looked around at the expectant faces. Our collective gaze focused on a lone candle attached to a pink ribbon tied to a diamond ring. Someone had gotten engaged. Sorority rules dictated the news be kept secret until the candle passing ceremony. The identity of the girl would be revealed when she blew out the candle.

As we all began to sing our sorority song, the president lighted the candle and passed it to the girl on her right. She passed it to the next girl, who passed it to the next.

The pattern continued until the candle stopped at a tall girl with long hair. She placed the ring on her finger and puffed on the flame, sending the room into a burst of congratulations. I joined the crowd surrounding Marissa and gave her a huge hug. I longed for the day my turn would come. My internal countdown ticked with each passing moment.

"We had another candle lighting ceremony," I casually mentioned to my boyfriend, Cameron, later when we studied together in the library. We'd recently started dating when he mentioned his interest to Collin, my protective running buddy and Cameron's best friend.

Everybody said we'd make such a cute couple, so I believed their words over my own feelings. Rather than attraction, I felt safe around Cameron, especially since he respected my desire to wait for sex until marriage. Weeks before my graduation, he came through with a ring so I could participate in the candle passing ceremony.

I couldn't wait to share the news. "Daddy, Cameron asked me to marry him." I thrust out my hand.

His frown jarred me.

"What's wrong, Daddy?"

"I'm sorry, Princess, but he's not the one."

"Oh, Daddy." I hugged his neck, dismissing his concern. "You can't be serious. Cameron listed all the reasons he loves me when he proposed."

I was a daddy's girl. Of course, he didn't want to see me leave the nest. This was the same father who flew home for 24 hours from a business trip in Poland for the sole purpose of watching me perform a routine with my high school drill team. His protectiveness was only natural.

I brushed aside his warning and began to plan my perfect wedding — an outdoor wedding in my parents' backyard on the banks of the Brazos River. My mother's beautiful flowers would accent the grounds filling the air with their fragrance.

Three months before the wedding, Cameron tried to break off our engagement, but I assured him things would be easier once I finished my graduate work. The long distance put too much stress on our relationship.

When my big day arrived, wedding music made my heart flutter. Ahead of me, my bridesmaids walked toward the minister.

"I love you, Daddy." I squeezed his arm as we waited for the processional to begin.

"It's not too late, Princess." He searched my eyes. "If you don't feel right, we can call everything off right now."

Deep down, I knew he was right, but I was too headstrong to give up, a perfectionist who had spent years compartmentalizing feelings while focusing on my goals.

かかか

If only I'd listened to my father. To the outsider, my honeymoon was perfect. Cameron and I had fun together in Jamaica.

But reality jolted me when I came home and no wedding details awaited my attention. The past several months had passed in a dream. *Was I really awake facing a long future with the wrong prince?*

I sat on our bed and bawled my eyes out. I'd made the biggest mistake of my life. And I was stuck.

Marriage was a sacred covenant before God. I'd seen the lifelong commitment made by both sets of grandparents and my parents.

Why hadn't I listened to my father? What could I do?

Hopeless, I fell back into old patterns. Feeling out of control, I had to take control of everything else. Exercise. Eating. My career path.

I finished my graduate studies in less than six months and accepted a job in human resources where I worked long hours, quickly impressing my boss and securing a promotion to management.

Cameron's job as an accountant was equally demanding, so I didn't complain at his odd hours, even when it meant he worked long into the night during the tax and fiscal seasons.

I longed for a deeper relationship, but I settled for the routine and thrust my energies into planning for the spacious home we decided to build in the upcoming suburban neighborhood of Carrollton.

Days passed into months. And months into a year. Then two years.

One night in August, Cameron and I sat on our back deck, admiring the expanse of stars above us. I chattered about a coworker's bridal shower I had attended earlier that day.

"I don't have a problem with homosexuality," Cameron suddenly blurted out.

My eyebrows furrowed at such a random comment. "I don't understand."

"It's late." Cameron stood up. "We'll talk more later. Let's go to bed."

The next night, we sat on our deck again when Cameron began the conversation. "I have to tell you something."

My stomach flip-flopped at the tone underlying his words.

"I've been with other men throughout our marriage."

My world faded to black. Scenes from my life flashed before me. My father's warning. Cameron's late nights and weekends. His lack of desire for me in bed.

I couldn't hear more. I rushed to the bathroom and stripped off my clothes. I had to wash off the filth. The betrayal.

"I'm so sorry," Cameron cried outside the door. "I didn't mean to hurt you."

"Leave me alone!" I screamed. "I don't want to see you."

I stepped into the shower. Tears ran from my eyes, blending with the scalding water beating my flesh. I balled my hands into fists and pounded the walls, screaming at both my foolishness and his infidelity.

Long after the water turned cold, I toweled off and called my former youth pastor.

"I don't know what to do," I shrieked into the phone.

Dan calmed down my hysteria. "Take a deep breath. Tell me what happened."

I blurted out the awful truth.

"God still loves you," he tried to reassure me. "He still has a plan for you."

I wanted to believe his words, but I couldn't. Cameron and I never agreed on a church to attend together, so I'd stopped going rather than sit alone.

"You gotta call my dad, Dan. I can't tell my parents."

He agreed, so I reluctantly hung up, terrified of my parents' condemnation. Daddy was speaking at a Christian Business Leaders conference in Florida. *How would he take the news?*

My hand trembled when I picked up the phone and heard my dad's voice. "I love you, Princess." Concern laced his voice. "Are you safe?"

"I don't know what to do, Daddy," I said through my tears. "You were right. I should never have married Cameron." I broke down on the phone.

"Shh, Princess." He didn't condemn me. "Pack up your bags and head to a hotel. Your mom and I will be on the first flight home tomorrow."

I grabbed a change of clothes and checked into a nearby Comfort Inn.

Unwelcome thoughts of Cameron's infidelity crept into my mind. I stripped down a second time and showered, longing to be free of the images assaulting my mind and clawing my body.

Sleep eluded me. I hated myself for being so stupid.

"Why, God?" I screamed into my pillow. "Why?"

Someone clomped around on the floor above me. *How could people continue living when my own life had stopped?*

"Why did you let this happen, God?" I clenched my fists. "What kind of a future awaits me?"

I screamed question after question, wrestling with God throughout the night. "I tried to be perfect." I cried long after the tears stopped. "A good girl."

I never expected perfection. I want your heart. Let me help you.

"Jesus, I need you," I breathed. "I'm so lost."

Clarity broke with my utterance for help. Two choices loomed before me: I could fall back on God, my foundation, or continue on my current path, trying to find fulfillment in my career, my new home, relationships and possessions.

"I feel so dry. So thirsty," I confessed. Nothing had brought real joy. Not like the God I once worshipped regularly. We used to talk all the time. Like when I was 15 at church camp and I heard him whisper his plans for my future.

"I choose you, Jesus," I whispered. "Please show me what to do now."

Dawn broke through the crack in the thick curtains.

Focus on me. Move out. Surround yourself with godly girlfriends.

The advice was so clear, I could almost feel God sitting next to me.

❧ ❧ ❧

I was an emotional wreck for two months. Cameron left, and my mom moved into my house to help me get it ready to sell. She listened to me for hours on end, never once judging me. I attended a support group and sought counseling from my youth pastor and his wife. I contacted a lawyer to annul our marriage.

When the house sold, I gave two weeks' notice to my bewildered boss and moved to Tulsa, Oklahoma, to be roommates with a friend who had recently lost her mother to cancer. We encouraged each other through our losses. I didn't waste any time finding a church to call home.

Forgive Cameron. I heard the familiar voice while I read a passage from the Bible one morning.

No, God, I refused. *He hurt me too bad.*

Hurting people hurt.

I wanted to plug my ears. Shut out God, but the request was a command. If I wanted complete healing, I needed to forgive.

Okay, God. Please help Cameron to find you. I know how miserable it is to be dying inside.

Better.

I wanted to roll my eyes at God.

Now pray for Cameron tomorrow.

What? I protested. *Remember what he did, God?*

Yes, so pray tomorrow. And the day after that.

You gotta be kidding.

No. I imagined God shaking his head. *Pray for Cameron and his family every day.*

I didn't feel like obeying, but I did it, anyway. By the third or fourth day, my heart started to change. God morphed my anger into compassion.

৵৵৵

"Come with me to Applebee's," my friend Kirstie begged me a few months later. "I need back up."

"Who's the guy?" I laughed.

"One of the bartenders. Damion." Her eyes sparkled. "We have a class together at Oral Roberts University, and I've had a crush on him forever. He's graduating this spring with a degree in multimedia and business."

"And he's single?"

"Finally." She pumped her arm in victory. "He and his girlfriend just broke up."

Damion was cute, but I wasn't the type to go after a friend's guy — even if his attention flattered me. I was far from ready to pursue another relationship.

"So, Dallas," Damion asked me. He couldn't remember my name, so he nicknamed me after the city I called home. "What are you girls doing after dinner?"

I shrugged.

"Going hot-tubbing," Kirstie piped up. "I'm house sitting, and they've got this great set-up out back. Why don't you and your roommate come over?"

Damion lit up. "Sounds fun."

Normally I'd shy away from something so vulnerable, but something about Damion made me agree. Later, as we talked, I was surprised to learn we attended different services at the same church.

I could see a good guy underneath the rough exterior, but Damion's foul mouth and addiction to cigarettes didn't match up with the recent list I'd made of qualities I desired in a future husband.

"So what's your story?" I asked him later when Kirstie and Damion's roommate were engaged in a conversation.

"I grew up as a pastor's kid, but rebelled when I left home. A few months ago, I told my parents I was going to ask my girlfriend, Serena, to marry me."

Pain shadowed Damion's face.

"I expected congratulations. Instead, they told me they'd pick up the pieces after our marriage fell apart."

"Sounds familiar." I hadn't yet told Damion about my failed marriage.

"I was furious and decided to marry her, anyway." Damion exhaled. "But they were right. We weren't meant for each other. I broke up with Serena last month. It was time someone challenged my choices. I've strayed a long way from God."

Brokenness welled in Damion's eyes.

"Obviously, I still need work." He pointed his cigarette. "But I told God I was ready to start over. If he didn't want me to date, then I'd wait."

I looked at the clock, surprised at the late hour. "I better go. It's been great talking."

"You should call me sometime," Damion said.

"I don't call guys."

He grinned. "Then give me your number. Maybe we can go to church together Sunday."

I raised my eyebrows. "Early service?"

"You're brutal." He groaned. "Making me get up after the late shift."

We met for church, and I invited him to a Bible study group the following Wednesday.

The more we talked, the more I knew Damion was the one for me. But this time I wanted my dad's blessing. I wouldn't make the same mistake and disregard his advice.

"Daddy," I called him a week later, "I've met this guy."

Silence made me cringe. I could imagine his lips tighten in disapproval.

"Isn't it too soon, Princess?"

"It took me by surprise, too, Daddy. I wasn't looking for a relationship."

He and Mom made the six-hour drive to Tulsa within a few short weeks.

Poor Damion. The guy wouldn't know what hit him.

My voice trembled as I introduced the two of them. They shook hands, and something sparked in my dad's eyes. I resisted the urge to scream, "Hallelujah!"

Daddy prayed over us and later admitted to me that he heard God whisper, *This is the one.*

I resolved not to fix Damion. If God wanted us to be together, he could do the changing. I began praying for God to change Damion's desire for cigarettes and foul language. Over Memorial Day weekend, Damion announced he was smoking his last cigarette.

"I want to get a tattoo to symbolize new beginnings."

"Really?" My eyes danced. "I was thinking the same thing. A butterfly would be the perfect symbol of transformation."

In July, my parents invited us to the Bahamas, so we met in Florida to meet Damion's parents. Our parents hit it off, further confirming our relationship. Like me, Damion wanted his parents' blessing before he asked for my hand in marriage.

Two weeks later, Damion and I went to an intimate fine-dining restaurant in Utica Square for his birthday. After strolling through a rose garden at Woodward Park, Damion led me to a private area under the trees where he set out a blanket and lit a candle. When he took out a ring box, my heart hammered in my chest.

He kneeled before me. "Will you marry me?"

"Yes!" I squealed.

He placed a ring on my trembling finger. It was too dark to see much, but I would marry Damion regardless of the size of the diamond.

We waited a full year after my annulment before we married at the small chapel at Rhema Bible College. This time God took center stage. Our dads recited the wedding vows, and my youth pastor, Dan, performed the ceremony. Our guests, family and close friends expressed their genuine joy at seeing our new beginning unfold together. Our honeymoon at a resort in Mexico couldn't have been more perfect.

❧ ❧ ❧

Three months later, I turned over in bed to find Damion missing. The blue light from the television beckoned me to the adjoining room. I pulled on my robe, not bothering to fix my tousled hair. Insecurities had loosened their grip on me since I'd begun praying regularly.

My smile turned to horror. Pornographic images on the screen assaulted me. Damion turned at the sound of my gasp.

"What are you doing?" I screeched and ran to the bathroom. Betrayal slammed a fist in my heart. I fell to the floor, sobbing uncontrollably. *This couldn't be happening.*

"Babe," Damion called outside the door. "I'm so sorry. I didn't mean to hurt you."

The irony of the scene playing out before me crushed me. I wailed even louder. *What was so wrong with me? Why wasn't I ever enough? First Cameron. Now Damion.*

"Please, babe." Damion leaned against the door. "Open up. Can we talk about this?"

"Go away!" I screamed. I wanted nothing to do with the lies.

He slumped to the floor. "I'm not leaving."

I refused to cave. I would not be a doormat.

Hours passed before I heard Damion leave. When I peered through the door, I saw he'd fallen asleep on the couch.

I tiptoed toward our bedroom and retreated into

silence the next morning. Damion tried to communicate, but I escaped to work, my getaway.

Later, when my emotions had settled, I listened to Damion confess his addiction to pornography. He grabbed my hands. "You gotta believe me. I don't want to hurt you."

Tears spilled from my eyes. "If we're going to make this work, we need a game plan." Damion nodded.

"No more cable," I insisted. "And we have to get rid of the computer."

He readily agreed, and we found a counselor and an accountability group at our church.

The test came a month later when I had to travel overnight for work.

"Were you able to stay faithful to your promise?" I asked him the next day, not even bothering with a greeting.

The shame on Damion's face made my heart sink. *Was our marriage doomed to fail?*

ॐ ॐ ॐ

Damion

I couldn't look Zoe in the face. I felt humiliated, powerless. *Help me, God. I'm going to lose my marriage if I can't sever this habit.*

I signed up for the next available *Every Man's Battle* workshop.

Thoughts of failure and inadequacy tortured me on the four-hour drive to McKinney, Texas. *How could I hurt the woman to whom I'd pledged my love?* She was beautiful — inside and out. Watching her suffer, I knew I couldn't let pornography poison our relationship.

The conference drew men from every walk of life — professionals, blue-collar workers, white, black, old, young. Our common addiction didn't discriminate. I'd never seen such vulnerability before. Discomfort made me want to leave several times throughout the workshop, but my commitment to Zoe kept me going to the break-out sessions. Heartbreaking stories of men losing everything — wives, kids, careers — jolted me awake. I stared at a future snapshot of myself. If I didn't want to end up the same, I needed to get serious about change.

I called my dad on the way home.

"I have a problem with pornography," I confessed.

He didn't reject me like I feared, but instead offered me encouragement. "Can I pray for you, son?"

Back home, I poured out my heart to Zoe, fully expecting her to embrace me with open arms. But her skepticism erected a wall. I had to work hard to earn back her trust.

The battle was far from easy, but talking to my counselor each week kept me accountable.

"I feel like there's a trigger. Something in your past that set you on this course." Johnny leaned back in his chair while we talked.

I shook my head. We'd been over this a dozen times in

the three or four months I'd been getting counseling. "There's nothing. I was raised in church."

Johnny eyed me. "Which means you learned how to save face. You said so yourself. Being a preacher's kid meant you had to act a certain way."

"Which explains my rebellion in college." I let out a frustrated sigh. "Not my addiction to pornography."

Johnny didn't back down. "What aren't you telling me?"

"Nothing!" I exploded.

Ragged breathing filled my ears when the memory blindsided me.

"What?" Johnny's voice faded.

Fuzzy details came into focus. "My brother and I spent the night with friends from church. Mom and Dad had something that kept them out late that night."

Johnny nodded for me to continue.

"They had two sons. My brother slept in the younger brother's room." A flash of memory made me pale.

"Something happened, didn't it?" Johnny's eyes softened.

I nodded. "I was only 12. I didn't understand what was happening to my body."

Johnny listened while I confided the details of the night I lost my innocence. Tears stained my face. "I was so afraid of my dad's reaction, I stuffed the memory."

Johnny let out a deep breath. "I'm sorry, Damion. That should've never happened."

I wiped at my eyes.

"The good news is we've found what triggered your addiction. To heal, you need to write a letter of forgiveness to your perpetrator."

"I don't even know his name."

Johnny brushed aside my concern. "You won't be giving the letter to him. The exercise is for you."

The next several months were some of the hardest in my life. Writing the letter forced me to confront pain I'd managed to forget for years.

After I read the letter to my accountability group at church, I shared it with Zoe. She held me until the tears stopped. "I'm so proud of you." She brushed my lips with a kiss.

Submitting to the painful process brought hope. Unexpected healing came when I put the words of forgiveness on paper. Finally, pornography lost its grip on me.

❧ ❧ ❧

"I'm not getting younger." Zoe looked at me across the pillow.

"So what are you saying?" I caressed her cheek. Our relationship had blossomed over the previous 15 months.

"That I'm ready to get a real house. This ghetto apartment is driving me crazy." She gave me a hopeful smile. "And we need to start thinking about our future family."

The more we talked, the more we realized we didn't

want to settle down in Tulsa. Neither of us liked the idea of raising our kids so far away from our families. We also wanted to be part of a church that felt like family where we could get involved serving at the ground level.

Zoe and I prayed for God's guidance and settled on La Quinta, California, where her parents had moved a year earlier.

Six months later, we pulled up to the house my in-laws were renting to us.

"Did we move to hell?" I swiped at the sweat running down my face.

Zoe unloaded another box off our Penske truck. "It's March. Why is it 115 degrees?"

Serious doubts began to plague me. *Had we misread God? Neither one of us even had a job here yet.*

We took a break and stepped into the kitchen where the contractor, a friend of Zoe's parents, was doing some work.

"It's not a coincidence God brought you here," Matt told us. "I want to introduce you to a friend."

A week later, Matt invited us to his house, along with Zoe's parents, to meet Pastors Eddie and Tammy. They shared their vision to start Champion Life Church in the valley and asked Zoe and me if we'd like to hear Pastor Eddie preach in Riverside the following Sunday.

Pastor Eddie's message on personal capacity touched me, reminding me of a favorite pastor in college, one of the few who didn't put me to sleep.

Helping birth a church put Zoe and me at the ground

level of ministry. I agreed to learn how to play an instrument, so I could be on the worship team, and Zoe helped with hospitality, technology and child care.

We couldn't wait to raise our kids at Champion Life, but a year after living in California, Zoe still hadn't gotten pregnant. She saw a specialist who prescribed her with medication, but another nine months passed without a baby.

Our church family kept growing, and their support was invaluable during the most discouraging days. They weren't just Sunday friends, they lived out Champion Life's motto: "Don't do life alone."

When our doctor wanted to explore further fertility options, we combined prayer with a 30-day fast where we gave up a meal to spend that extra time in prayer to hear God's plans for our future family.

Should we adopt? Should we try another form of fertility treatment? Since some of these methods are controversial, we really wanted to hear God's desire for our family.

Our answer came in the form of in vitro fertilization. In December, Zoe got the news that she was pregnant. We were ecstatic. The doctor cautioned us against telling people, but we insisted upon sharing the news with our church family. We wanted this baby covered in prayer.

Hope arrived on September 1, 2009, four years after we'd begun praying for her. When I didn't hear her cry, I held my breath. Then, to my amazement, she sneezed three times.

"Hope's definitely a daddy's girl." Zoe beamed at me. "She sneezes in threes like you."

Daddy's girl.

The words swelled my heart with joy.

৵৵৵

A busy, happy year disappeared in a flurry of diapers and interrupted nights. Our desire for another baby prompted Zoe and me to begin prayer and fasting.

Thirty days later, on the last day of our fast, a social worker called me. "Your cousin is expecting again," she told me. "She can't take care of the baby. How would you feel about adopting her child?"

I could hardly contain my excitement. Zoe echoed my feelings.

Because the baby had yet to be born, we faced some hurdles with the adoption process. God moved on our behalf, amazingly cutting the two-year process in half. But still the waiting process drained us, taking Zoe and me on a different kind of labor and delivery journey.

Baby Grace arrived a day after Christmas in 2010 and was placed in a foster home for three months. While the family members were loving Christians, we were happy when my parents took over Grace's care.

Zoe and I didn't shy away from being vulnerable with our struggles and heartache. We refused to let the negativity or doubts get a grip on our lives and pressed into our church family at Champion Life for prayer and support. They rallied alongside us during the long days we awaited custody.

Pastor Eddie, knowing our hearts, asked if the two of us would train to be facilitators for a program called Celebrate Recovery. Even with the promise of busy days ahead, Zoe and I readily agreed. We wanted to help others find the same freedom we'd found.

In August, the long-awaited day finally arrived. Zoe and I stepped off the plane with 8-month-old baby Grace to find our church family had filled the airport, holding bouquets of balloons and welcome home signs.

I looked over at Zoe and felt the tears well in my eyes. We were parents. Again.

I kissed her head. "Congratulations, Mommy."

She squeezed my hand and looked toward heaven.

God had answered her prayers … and mine.

ৡৡৡ

Three months later, we launched Celebrate Recovery at Champion Life. While we adapted to busy days with two young girls, God began using Celebrate Recovery to bring hope to some of the first participants. Former drug addicts, Rich and Nellie, found freedom from addiction, while Raul and Maria found hope for a marriage failing due to his multiple affairs.

As Grace's first birthday neared, my parents planned a January visit. Pastor Eddie agreed to dedicate Grace to God during their stay with us.

Standing together with our parents and surrounded by our church family, we vowed to raise Grace to know her loving heavenly father. We'd made the same promise with Hope.

"Children are a heritage from the Lord," Pastor Eddie quoted Psalm 127. "A reward from him."

Zoe met my gaze. The thought both overwhelmed me with gratitude and humbled me at the task of fatherhood before me.

God handpicked our girls for us. Hope and Grace were our heritage and reward.

I breathed a prayer for help, grateful for my heavenly father's leading … and forever indebted to him for new beginnings.

THE ROAD OF ENDURANCE
The Story of Cindy
Written by Alexine Garcia

"Do you mind if we stop by my house? I need to pick up a few things," I asked Kelly from the backseat. My friend Jazmine sat in the back next to me.

"Sure, it's on the way, anyway," she answered with white knuckles clenched on the steering wheel. She was still nervous about learning to drive. Thankfully, her mom sat next to her in the passenger seat, keeping her calm and focused.

She pulled into my driveway, and I slid the van door open. It was a beautiful sunny day. I walked up the front porch and saw the white grocery bag hanging from the doorknob. My mom had folded everything I needed for the day. There was just one last thing she forgot: my blue binder. I unlocked the door and went down the hall to my room.

My mother's bedroom door was open, and as I looked in, shock swept over my body like a rush of cold wind. I was stuck staring into the eyes of a man lying on top of my mother. He quickly jumped off the bed and ran to the bathroom. My mom and I locked eyes, and it felt like time stopped ticking. I broke free from the paralysis and darted into my room.

I stared at the ceiling trying to catch my breath. Finally, I snapped out of it. I didn't even grab my binder. I just ran out of the house and slammed the door behind me.

"Are you okay?" Jazmine asked me with a look of concern on her face. I couldn't get any words out and just sat looking out the window.

"You look as white as a ghost. Did you and your mom get in a fight?"

Kelly, nervous about driving the car, didn't think much of it and pulled out of the driveway. Her mom looked back at me worried. Kelly was unfamiliar with my neighborhood and took a wrong turn. As we came back around the block I saw the man, this time clothed, jogging down the street away from our house. My pulse pounded in my ears, and that morning's breakfast began to rise in my throat. I placed my hand over my mouth as I started to gag.

"We're here," Kelly's mom said, reaching for her purse. As I stepped out of the van onto the asphalt, my legs gave way beneath me. I collapsed and began to hyperventilate. Kelly's mom helped me up and held me close as we walked to the bathroom.

"Go get Pastor Susan," she said to Jazmine.

I paced through the restroom feeling dizzy and nauseous. When the youth pastor, Susan, came into the restroom, I felt my heart clench up. How was I supposed to explain something I myself could hardly believe? A wave of shock choked me up, and it was a good 10 minutes before I could get any words out.

She hugged me tight and walked me to the head

pastor's office. I picked up the phone and called my mother.

"Mom … I don't want you here today," I told her.

"Are you sure that's what you want, honey?"

"Yes, Mom. I'm really upset about what I saw, but I don't want this to get in the way of something so important."

"All right, I'll see you when you get home."

I hung up the phone and sat quietly with Pastor Susan before she finally asked me, "Do you want to call your father?" I knew it had to be done. I picked up the phone and dialed his cell phone number. He had been staying with family while my parents were discussing a separation. They had been apart only four days, and my dad had already told my brother he would be home very soon.

"Hello," he answered. I was so nervous I was shaking. "Hello?"

"Dad, it's me, Cindy. I need to tell you something," I whispered as tears began to roll down my face. He waited quietly for me to go on. "I saw … I witnessed something I shouldn't have at home. You should probably call Mom."

"Are you okay, sweetie? Where are you?"

"I'm at church."

"I'm coming over. I'll see you in a bit."

It was not easy telling my dad what I saw. He spoke with my mom. It turned out she had been with that man, Brandon, for a year and a half. My dad never got to come home like he planned. Instead, they went through with a divorce.

❧❧❧

My brother went to live with my dad, and I stayed with my mom. My emotions were like a tangled ball of yarn that I had no idea how to untie. Before the divorce I didn't have any desire to drink. But something just snapped in me, and alcohol and partying became a way to suppress the pain. Pain was an awful, terrible thing to me, and it only caused problems I didn't need. When I was drunk with my friends at the weekend parties, or even in my own living room, I didn't have to think about any of it. I just wanted to feel numb. Emotions were for losers.

In January of 1997, I went on a weekend trip with the youth group. We spent time reading the Bible, playing outdoor games and, of course, we had late-night girl talks from our bunk beds. We talked about the things we couldn't bring up in the main group sessions.

"Well, I just can't believe God allowed my parents to divorce," I said bitterly to the girls.

Pastor Susan answered me right away. "God tells us in the book of James to be joyful when we face trials. The testing of our faith produces patience."

I sat straight up in my bunk and snapped, "*Joy*? I'm supposed to have joy about all this? I walked in on my mom sleeping with a man. My parents are divorced. And my brother doesn't even want to live with us. How is this supposed to be joyful?"

"Well, God teaches us lessons we will need in life through trials."

"That doesn't make any sense, Pastor."

"Sometimes the only way God can truly reach us is through the hard times. He makes us stronger, and we learn perseverance with each issue we face. Perseverance means the ability to endure hardship. On top of all that, we grow closer to God in the middle of our struggles."

I felt so closed off to what she was saying and rolled over in my sleeping bag. "None of this makes sense. I'm going to sleep." My first reaction was to cry, but I didn't want these people to see that side of me. Tears were weakness, and I certainly was not weak.

"Cindy, I know that this has caused you so much pain, but I want to urge you to grow close to God. He has so much to teach you during this time."

Her words stung, but I knew they were true.

ॐॐॐ

Back at home I sat in my room thinking over everything I had learned on the trip. There was no alcohol to help me cope with my emotions, and I sat at the edge of my bed face to face with my feelings. Pastor Susan's words would not leave me alone. As I began to let go of my anger, it felt like unclenching a fist. I took a deep breath and slid down to my knees and sobbed into my pillow.

"God, I'm so angry at you! I don't know how you could let this happen. Our family is torn apart. My emotions are a mess. These past few months have felt like hell in this home, and I don't know why you are allowing all of this. Most of all, I don't know how to handle all this. I know it's going to be hard, but I forgive my mother."

In that moment, warm relief washed over me. I could actually feel a heaviness lift off my shoulders. I took a deep breath and opened my eyes. I made a plan to talk to her when she got home.

My heart pounded wildly in my chest as I watched my mom walk in the front door that evening. I could almost hear my pulse in my head. Doubt crept in. *Am I doing the right thing? How will she react? Will she be defensive? What if she just rationalizes her actions?* Despite my doubts, I knew what I had to do.

"Mom, I need to talk to you." She looked at me and could see that this was something serious.

"Sure, honey." We sat on the couch in the living room.

I closed my eyes and took a deep breath. "I've been praying, Mom. And I know this is what God wants me to do. I love you. You're my mom, and I will always love you. But you hurt me. I've been so angry with you … but I forgive you for what you did. This doesn't mean that I'm okay with Brandon. I don't like him, and I don't want him to be my stepfather. I just know that I love you, and I need to forgive you." Tears ran down her face, and she grabbed me in a hug.

"Thank you, Cindy. I love you, too." We sat there hugging and crying, and I knew what I had to do next. Pastor Susan had been telling me about the bitterness that unforgiveness causes in our lives, and I could see it forming in me like weeds blooming on a beautiful lawn.

Even though I had forgiven my mom and the weight was lifted, I had to forgive Brandon. I knew my feelings toward him were the root of my anger.

Even telling my mom made me shake inside. "I forgive him, too, Mom. I will tell him if I see him again." She was happy I was taking this step, and she felt a bit of relief herself. The thick cloud of tension and grief was slowly clearing from our home.

A few weeks later, I came home from school, and my mom greeted me at the door. This was unusual, so I knew something was up.

"He's here," she whispered, pointing to the kitchen. I was glad she waited a few weeks to bring him over, but it didn't make it easier. Sweat began to build on my palms, and my legs felt shaky. I walked to my room to gather my thoughts and get a hold of myself. I didn't want to forgive him, but I reminded myself of the horrible bitterness that would return if I didn't.

I walked into the kitchen and looked at him sitting at the table. He didn't greet me or say hello. He was a bit of a mousy man. He had curly salt-and-pepper hair and a beer belly. What my mother saw in that chubby face was beyond me. My mind went back to that day I watched him jogging down our street. The same reaction returned to my body, and I felt my food rising up from my stomach. I took deep breaths as I sat down across from him. I knew what I had to say, but the words were caught in my throat. Tears began to build as I sat shaking, looking straight into his face. He didn't return my gaze.

"I have to do this for myself. And I'm not saying I'm always going to be nice to you or that this isn't going to be hard, but I forgive you."

"Thank you," he said in his mousy voice. He looked down into his lap and whispered, "I'm sorry." His words lacked sincerity, but I accepted his apology.

Somehow my mom thought this meant she could bring him over more often. Looking at him was hard. Trying to not blame him for my family disaster was not easy. I had to constantly remind myself that I forgave him each time my anger rose like bile in my throat.

Forgiveness was one thing, but watching my mom with Brandon was painful. Thankfully, I found an escape, or so I thought. I flew to Idaho right after graduation and attended a church summer camp. I was offered a job at the camp and accepted.

I returned home and began planning. I put in my two weeks' notice at the gymnastics center where I worked, but somehow my coworker Alice convinced me to turn down the job and stay with her instead. She helped me get a promotion, and I thought things were really looking up.

❧ ❧ ❧

"Wake up, Cindy!" Alice said, throwing my bedroom door open. Little rays of light snuck through the closed shutters. The clock read 7:30. I got up and threw on my slippers and robe before walking down the hall to her room.

I knocked, and she quickly answered, "Come in." She was rolling weed inside a zigzag as I walked in. I quickly fell right in sync with the morning routine of living with Alice: wake up, smoke a joint, get ready for work. The after-work routine was just as appealing with endless rounds of beer and liquor. Sometimes her parents even joined in. The freedom was intoxicating. I didn't have to deal with my emotions in this place. I could float away from reality for a bit, except for the times that Alice felt the need to bring up my personal problems.

"So what's up with your dad calling all the time?" she asked while she lit up. I waited for her to pass me the joint, anxious about answering her question. She took her time taking several puffs of the joint.

"He's trying to stay in touch with me. He actually cares, you know." I finally took the joint from her hand as she held it out between her thumb and middle finger. That first morning puff always felt the best.

"You know, you barely even look like him. Are you sure with the way your mom acts that he is even your dad?" Her tongue was razor sharp, and sometimes I even wondered if she had emotions. I hid my hurt feelings, while blowing out a cloud of smoke.

"What do you mean? Of course, he's my dad."

"Whatever," she said as I passed her the joint again.

Each day was just like the one before. Weed in the morning. Working the afternoon. Drinking at night. Days began to mesh, and my life slowly became a blur. At first the freedom was nice, but I was beginning to watch my life pass me by as I sat in my cloud of smoke and oblivion. Every night it was the same crowd of friends. I pretended to have a good time as we smoked and drank our beers in Alice's garage. But, really, I was envious of their smiles and laughter.

ॐॐॐ

"That Halloween party was crazy," David said while looking over the beer choices.

"I thought I was going to be all scared with that movie you guys put on, but it ended up being a good trip," Sharron said. We were at the grocery store getting stocked up for the night.

Alice nudged me with her bag of red plastic cups. "We still have a few hits of acid left that we're going to finish up tonight."

I tried to ignore her hints, but she kept persisting. "Try it with us."

"I'll be good with this six-pack," I said, grabbing my Sierra Nevada. I began to imagine what it would be like if one of them caused a ruckus and we all got caught on this bad acid trip. The thought of red and blue lights flashing in her front yard brought a twinge of anxiety.

As the sun set and the garage filled with tendrils of smoke, I began to relax. They had dropped their acid, and they weren't going crazy, so perhaps this would be fun after all. I already made it through one joint and two drinks, and I was feeling good.

"C'mon, Cindy, I saved you a hit," Alice said with a smirk.

I looked up at the ceiling covered in a haze of smoke. At this point, the fuzzy carefree feeling set in, and I agreed. We walked down the block together, and I was amazed at how beautiful the night looked. Each streetlamp and traffic light gleamed with brilliant rays of light. I had to remain composed and not break into the giggles since we were out in public. Back at the garage we watched *The Matrix*, and Alice's mother joined us. It was a pleasant experience that I took part in several more times. After trying acid, ecstasy was an easy yes.

Amidst all the chaos, I continued to meet up with my dad every other week. He was under the impression that I had a good job, friends and a responsible lifestyle.

"Why do you even bother with your family?" Alice asked me as I walked in the front door after our visit. If I hadn't been so naïve, I could have recognized her jealousy and manipulation. Instead, I let her words cut deep.

"They're my parents."

"And your mom? Is she still with that fat loser? You need to stop visiting them. Let them see what life would be like without you." I looked down at my feet as I left the kitchen. I didn't want her to see the effect her words had on me.

I fell back onto my bed and stared at the ceiling. I had come here to get away from my mom and Brandon. I was so eager to get away that I didn't see what I was getting myself into. My relationship with my parents was almost nonexistent. And now a new thought materialized in my mind. I was just as miserable here as I was in my mom's house. My friendship with Alice was rich with envy, manipulation, anger, drugs and chaos.

I began planning to move out to Palm Desert to live with my aunt, but I had no idea what to tell Alice. A few weeks later, I gathered up the guts to talk to her.

I told her I was moving with my mom to help her financially, when I really only planned to stay with Mom long enough to save for my move to Palm Desert. Alice didn't ask a lot of questions. And that was that. I had expected an argument or some sort of manipulation to get me to stay. But perhaps Alice was just never sober enough to care.

෴෴෴

I packed up my white sedan and headed home. When I got home, Mom didn't seem to care. It was like I was just getting home from any other day.

That same night she took me to her favorite bar. Cathy, the owner, welcomed my mom with her favorite drink.

"Cathy, this is my daughter, Cindy." I greeted her and shook her hand. The dark bar was filled with laughter, loud karaoke and the click of balls rolling across the pool table. As I looked into the mirror behind the bar, I could see my unhappy reflection. After suppressing my feelings for so long, I was beginning to wonder if I had any left. As my mom's friends began filling the bar, it was obvious that I was the youngest person there. For some reason, this helped me relax a little.

"Here, sweetie," my mom said, pushing a beer across the table nonchalantly. That one bottle turned to four before the end of the night, and a fake smile was painted across my face. I felt more at ease here. I didn't have to watch what I said for fear of Alice's ridicule. Plus, they were my mom's friends, not mine. Somehow that made it all easier. I also appreciated the fact that my mom smoked weed. It was something we started doing together every day.

The next night the same crowd brought the party to the house. It was nice not worrying about driving. The more I got to know these people, the more I relaxed. The fact that Brandon came around less often was nice, too.

"How long are you planning on staying?" my mom asked, while aiming at the dartboard.

"I was thinking a few weeks. I want to move out to Palm Desert with Aunt Beth," I replied. I threw my dart and missed completely.

"You'll get better. It takes practice," she said. "You know, Cathy said you could work as a server at the bar."

"Is that even legal?"

"Yeah, you're 18. Why not? You won't be bartending, not at first, anyway. Then after your shift we could party just like yesterday." Her darts all landed in the inner circle despite her drunken swagger. "Think about it, and let me know if you change your mind." She walked over to her friends and took a joint from an older balding man's hand. Watching my mom act this way made me realize why she was lenient with me growing up. Now I realized that she was out doing the same things I was. How could she tell me not to?

Working at the bar was just as much fun as my mom said it was. Even so, I took on a second job at a restaurant to make extra cash.

I was having a great time, and I had just about forgotten about Alice. My troubles with anxiety were all gone. But the more fun we had, the more I realized that I was still living in a cloud.

My mom, Cathy and I took a trip out to Santa Cruz to hit the beach for a day. The weather was so bright and perfect for a beach trip. I rolled down the window and let the wind whip through my hair.

"Don't get too comfortable just yet," my mom said. "I need to stop at the office and grab something right quick." She pulled into the parking lot of the empty building and ran in.

"I know exactly what she's grabbing right quick," Cathy said with a chuckle.

"What is it?" I asked. Cathy didn't answer, and I quickly forgot.

The weather was even prettier out at Santa Cruz. We sat on the beach, and I swam in the ocean and watched the surfers catch the waves. The boardwalk was packed with people, but it didn't stop our fun. It was amusing to flirt and smile at the passing faces. We sat on the patio of a crab shack and drank beer to our heart's content.

"Are we still going bowling after this?" Cathy asked, while fixing her lipstick after the meal. The nice buzzed feeling crept over me after my third beer, and bowling sounded really fun.

"Yeah, I just have to stop by the car first." The two exchanged a quick smirk, and I knew they were up to something.

The sun was setting as we walked to the car. The sky was painted with bright hues of orange and pink. My mom popped the trunk and pulled a small baggy of yellowish-white powder from her workbag.

"I knew it!" Cathy said as her eyes lit up.

"What is that?"

"It's just a little something to keep us awake," she said as my mom took a line through a small straw. Cathy took a turn, too, and my mom looked me in the eyes.

"Try it."

"Oh, no. No, I've never done that before."

"Just do one line. It will keep you up the entire night." And one line of that powder was all it took for me to love it. Meth was my mom's drug of choice, and so it was easy to get. With my sleep pattern out of whack and living in a constant haze, I began to yearn for reality. But I wasn't happy if I was sober. My face didn't even look familiar in the mirror anymore.

I was cleaning my room when I came across a photo from my senior year, before the drugs and alcohol got out of hand. The smiling girl in the picture hanging out with all her friends didn't look like someone I knew. My heart clenched into that familiar fist as I realized that I had done this to myself. I threw the frame at the floor, and the glass shattered all over the tile. I had come here to get away from myself, and I only dove deeper into darkness. It was time to move to Aunt Beth's place.

My old friend Cassie decided it would be nice to throw me a going-away birthday party. That same day my dad and brother wanted to take me out to dinner.

I snorted my seven daily lines of speed that day before getting ready for the night. I curled my hair in the bathroom, thinking hopeful thoughts about my move. This was going to be a fresh start. As soon as I got away, I could kick the drug habit.

I suddenly woke up on the bathroom floor. I didn't even remember the moment I passed out. I shook off the dizzy feeling and got to my feet. A wave of fear rushed over my body like a cold chill as I looked in the mirror. A stream of blood flowed down my face from each nostril. *How did this happen? Were my lines too fat tonight? Was the meth laced with something?* There was no telling. My thoughts only increased the dizzy feeling. I washed my face and removed the caked blood. I didn't know how long I had been on the floor. *I just need a few chugs of beer to get my head straight,* I thought to myself. I only had 30 minutes before meeting with my dad, and I really had to pull myself together.

I was relieved when neither of them seemed able to tell

anything was wrong. The makeup had covered my pale face. I ate a few bites of salad as we carried on small talk. I felt very far from them, even though I was only sitting across the table. *This move will be a fresh start,* I reassured myself.

We hugged, and I choked back tears as I realized how far away I was moving from my family. I could see Dad's eyes fill with tears before I walked away.

At the going-away party, I was still shaken up by what the drugs had done to me. I managed to stay away from meth the rest of the night. The image of my reflection and blood-smeared face kept coming back to mind.

I excitedly packed my belongings the next morning. I started up the car engine and immediately began daydreaming about the fresh start I was making.

Driving eight hours away was the perfect start to get away from the drugs. My aunt went to a really good church, and perhaps I could get back in touch with God.

The thought of God brought a sudden stream of regret to mind. How did I let myself get here? Almost two years ago, I had knelt in my room, feeling like God was right next to me. Now I was so far from that moment. I realized that it was a slow, steady slope I traveled down. This all started when I turned down the job in Idaho and chose Alice and weed over God. Moving in with my mom brought meth into my life. And now I had to drive eight hours away to try and get my life straight.

Those same eight hours would be a huge distance

between my dad and brother and I. Emotions flooded my thoughts, and I struggled to see the road through the blur of tears.

I made it as far as my grandma's house as the sun was setting. The next morning I woke up refreshed and ready to finish the last two hours of the trip. I was ready to leave everything behind me and start over. I had been transferred to a different location of the same restaurant chain, which I was thankful for. I needed to keep myself busy and away from drugs. The image of my blood-smeared face would not leave me alone.

As I pulled up to the house in Palm Desert, my aunt came out to greet me.

"Well, it looks like you made good time. I am so happy you're here," she said, grabbing me into a hug. "Let me help you with your bags."

"Thank you. I didn't really bring much."

My room was small, but it had all the furniture and closet space I needed. The next morning I went to meet my new manager. Walking into the same smells and atmosphere was a bit comforting and surreal. I wouldn't have to learn any new menu items or routines. The idea of new coworkers and starting over was really exciting.

I started back to work three days later and fell right into place with the routine. I could see that I would have to get used to a lot of new faces and the regular customers, but that was never a problem for me. After a few months, I was already making new friends. My new coworker Derrick took me snowboarding with his friends on several occasions, and I often hung out with the other waitresses after work. The bartender, Brian, often hung out with us after work for a few drinks.

One night I was invited to Derrick's girlfriend's house. She worked at Applebee's, too. Perhaps if I were really serious about quitting the drugs, I would have just gone home, but I decided to join them.

Debbie's apartment was small and cozy. We sat around listening to music, drinking beer and smoking cigarettes. Debbie came over and sat on the couch next to me.

"So I hear you're from Palm Springs," she said after taking a swig from her bottle.

"Yeah, I'm living with my aunt now. I came down to make some changes in my life. I was pretty heavy into drugs."

"Oh, really? I just got out of a sober living home. I know how it is."

Debbie seemed nice enough. Her apartment was only a few blocks from work, which made it a good hangout spot.

Some of Debbie's friends came over and discretely sold her some meth. No one else seemed to notice, but I knew exactly what was going on.

"So who were they?" I asked her with a smirk.

"Oh, those are just some friends of mine. They came to drop some stuff off," she said casually. I knew exactly what she meant.

"Oh, I see," I said with a sly smile. "Just some stuff, huh?"

"Yeah," she replied, laughing. "You want to check it out?"

"Sure."

I was back at it again. The next two weeks I was getting speed regularly from Debbie. We hung out occasionally and did the drug together.

"Hey, Derrick. What's up with Debbie? I didn't see her at work today."

"Yeah, she had to quit."

"Is she all right?"

"She's okay. She's just going back into rehab."

I was shocked. "I know this probably leaves you high and dry," he said. "She didn't really tell me anything, either, if it makes you feel better."

Luckily, she had introduced me to the people who sold to her. I continued to use every day, working hard to keep my dangerous secret.

Not long after I moved to Palm Desert, I got a second job at a pizza place. I found myself hanging out for drinks after most of my shifts. I could tell that a coworker Calvin had his eye on me.

At work one night, I sat down at a barstool in the kitchen with a few girls playing a card game when Calvin walked up to me with a drink. "When are we going to go out?" he asked, popping open another beer for me.

"Calvin, you know how busy I am. I work two jobs."

"Let's just get together and have some fun. How about you come over tomorrow for dinner and some drinks?"

"I will come over if you agree that we are just friends. This is not going to be a date or anything like that."

He smirked and took a swig from his beer. "Sure."

His apartment was close to my aunt's house, so I could easily duck out if things went south. He bought Chinese takeout and a huge amount of beer.

"Is this 24-pack just for the two of us? Are you *trying* to get me drunk?"

"Don't be silly. I like to stock up and have them in the fridge in case friends come over. Kinda like you here tonight." I downed them one after another and lost count after seven. Calvin ended up being good company. He knew how to keep the conversation going and kept me laughing.

I woke up before the sun in his bed with my head still spinning. I quietly rolled out of the bed and felt around the dark floor for my clothes.

"What are you doing?" he said in a husky whisper. I knew he had consumed even more of that pack than I had.

"I need to sneak back in before my aunt notices. I'll see you tomorrow," I lied.

Even if he was nice, I didn't have any intentions of taking this relationship anywhere. I wasn't interested in keeping a boyfriend around. Especially not someone who would sleep with me the first time we hung out together.

It was a Friday night, and the restaurant was packed with a line of five different parties waiting. It didn't look like the evening rush hour would end anytime soon. The hostess was busy, so I sat a couple at the bar with menus.

"Thanks, Cindy," Brian said with a wink. He was always happy to get more customers. He was a hard worker, and people really liked his charisma. I circled the restaurant, visiting each of my tables, making sure my customers were doing well. I could see that the busboys were fixing up another table in my section. Brian stopped me on my way to the back to check my orders.

"Hey, are you going to Julie's tonight?"

"I wasn't planning on it. I have an early shift tomorrow."

"You should at least hang out for a bit." Brian had started taking an interest in me. I didn't feel any attraction to him. He was 10 years older, and he was going to school studying psychology. I didn't think we had much in common, but every time we hung out, he could hold an interesting conversation. Even though he partied with the rest of us, I knew Brian was searching for God.

That night I took his advice and went out with the group. I found myself laughing over a few beers with Brian. He was easygoing, and I realized that I could open up to him.

"How did you end up here in Palm Desert?" he asked.

"I came to live with my aunt. Life was getting pretty crazy back home, so I came here to get away. I'm not really sure things are any different here, though."

"What do you mean? What was so bad about back home?"

"Well, I was really heavy into meth."

"Wow. That's the hard stuff. When you say things are no different here, do you mean that you're still doing it?"

"I didn't plan on getting back into it. One thing just led to another. I guess us users kind of attract each other."

"You're talking about Debbie, huh? You know she's in some rehab trying to get her life straight?"

I took a drink from my beer, and we sat in awkward silence.

"You know, you have so much potential. And as good as rehab is, nothing can really change a person like God can." My breath caught in my throat as he mentioned God. I hadn't talked about God, much less been to church, in so long.

"My aunt goes to a pretty good church."

"Well, there's a start. And you don't even have to go alone. You really should go with her." I appreciated his kindness and his encouragement. It was nice to see a guy talk about God so openly. Most guys that talked to me had other thoughts on their minds.

Three weeks later, I sat on the edge of the toilet staring at two pink lines. This was the last thing I needed.

"Life happens," my dad said after a long silence. I had called him first because I knew he would be more understanding than my mom.

"Come to San Jose, and stay here with your brother and me. We have a guest room. We can figure this out one day at a time."

I wasn't sure if this was what I wanted to do, but it was

nice to have my dad's help. We had come so far in our relationship, and I didn't want to lose it now.

Telling my aunt was a much harder task. The color left her face as we sat across from each other at the dinner table.

"I'm going to go back home and live with my dad in a few weeks. I talked to him last night."

I was sitting at the bar a few weeks later, waiting for Kim to get off as I watched Brian make a Long Island Iced Tea. "Do you want me to make you anything?"

"Nah. Not tonight. I'm going to quit for a while."

"Yeah, I bet you are," he said, smirking. He put a straw in the drink and handed it to a lady at the other end of the bar.

"I have to quit for about nine months, actually."

His eyes popped open. "Who knocked you up?" blurted from his mouth.

"It was just a friend from my other work."

"Wow. What a friend." We laughed as Kim sat in the seat next to me. "Where are you two heading?"

"I'm dropping Kim off with the others, and I'm going to head home."

"That's good. I guess your life will be calming down a bit now."

"Yeah, it sure looks that way. I'm going to move back with my dad in San Jose."

I saw the disappointment in his face. We had started hanging out more often, and he was trying to help me get clean. I could see that he liked me.

The next morning my phone rang. I was surprised to hear both my mom and dad on the other line.

"Are you guys together?" The thought of them in the same house struck me as odd.

"No, we are on a three-way call," my mom said. There was a long silence before my dad spoke up.

"We're calling about your pregnancy."

"Yeah, I'm getting things in order to come back home."

"That's what we need to talk to you about," my mom said in a nervous voice.

"Your mother and I have talked about this. We have decided that we just cannot support you if you go through with this." My dad was strongly against abortion, and I knew that somehow my mom was influencing him. I had no words to say to them. My mind was like a chalkboard wiped clean.

"Honey?" The nervousness in her voice turned to a whisper.

"Okay. Well, I'm going to go. I have to figure things out." My dad was my only option. I didn't have the money to live on my own and take care of hospital bills, much less a child.

A week later my cousin was driving me to an abortion clinic two hours away. I bent my head down and watched my feet walk forward as we passed picketers in the parking lot. I tuned out their chants and looked away from their gruesome posters. The clinic was cold and white. I sat in a cubicle, while a nurse asked me questions in a monotone voice. It was like any other routine visit. It reminded me of getting my driver's license at the DMV.

"I need your signature here to prove your consent."

The ride home was silent. My cousin respected my need to sit in silence, so she turned the volume up on the radio. I leaned my head against the window and watched miles of office buildings, strip malls and gas stations pass by. I didn't let myself feel any emotion. Two days later, I went right back to work. Life went back to normal for the next few months, and people were under the impression that I had a miscarriage.

❧❧❧

After a long night of partying at another coworker's place, we were all wasted. I had done two lines at the beginning of the night and was wide awake. I could tell Brian probably needed a ride.

"I'll drive you," I said. He didn't even blink as he handed me his keys. It was fun watching him stagger into the passenger seat of his own car. I was wide awake as I drove us back to the street where my car was.

"You should probably leave your car at work and let me drive you home."

"Yeah. I don't mind. Are you sure you're not too tired?" He looked over at me and realized how sober and energetic I looked, even after downing just as many drinks as he had. "When was the last time you did speed, Cindy?"

I pulled the car into a parking spot as I fumbled

through my mind for an answer. I just couldn't lie to him. I was starting to like him just as much as he liked me. "Tonight."

He looked down into his lap and let out a sigh. "Oh, Cindy ..."

I pulled the baggy from my purse and looked at the pile of crystals for the last time. I opened the car door and emptied the bag onto the concrete. "It will be the last," I said with a smile. I could tell he didn't believe me.

The same sense of relief I'd had when I sobbed while kneeling at the edge of my bed so many years before washed over me. I didn't know how all of this was going to work out, but suddenly, somehow, I knew God would take care of it.

"I know this is what God wants for your life, and you can do it, Cindy," Brian said kindly. "If you need any help, I will be here for you. I can help you find a rehab or whatever it is you need."

I drove home that morning with a feeling of complete peace. I went to sleep and woke up that afternoon. Steve, my cousin's boyfriend, was at the house. He had overcome a speed addiction, and I knew he could help me.

"I need to talk to you about something."

"What's up?" he asked.

"I quit speed. Today."

He stopped what he was doing and sat at the edge of the bed. "You're just going to do cold turkey, no treatment?"

"Yeah, I guess so."

"All right, then. You can do this, but it's not going to be easy."

I didn't believe him when he said the symptoms would start right away, but they did. I was puking every 30 minutes. The next day I opened up to my aunt, and she offered to help me through it. I was too sick for the next week to be thankful. My headaches felt like hammers pounding on my head. Every time I attempted to eat, I threw up. I wanted to crawl out of my skin. I was desperate for some kind of relief from the shaking and intense chills.

I woke up to the sound of my phone buzzing. "Hello?"

"You're alive," Brian said.

"Yes, I think I'm going to make it." I still had a headache, but I could finally feel the violent sickness lifting.

"Well, I'll let you get some rest. I just wanted to check on you. You should probably crack open your Bible and start reading. That will help you get through this."

The next Sunday, I returned to church. The Sunday after that I went again, and soon church became a part of my life again. It felt like my life was falling back into place.

"You know, it's been awesome seeing you come this far," Brian said to me over the phone one night. I had stopped going out to drink after work, and so had he. My conversations with Brian were more comforting than beer. I began to realize that God could help me through my emotions better than any drug or drink. Sometimes it was more painful, but in the end I learned the value of perseverance and character that God had tried to teach me on that retreat so long before.

"Why don't I read you some verses while you fall asleep?" Brian said one night.

"Sure." I put the phone on speaker and turned out the lights.

"In the beginning was the Word, and the Word was with God, and the Word was God …"

❧ ❧ ❧

I was clearing my last table when Brian walked up to me. "You almost ready?"

"Sure." It was Valentine's Day 2002, and I was excited to give him his surprise. We had started spending more time hanging out and less time drinking.

He was about to put on a movie in his room when I got the card out of my purse. "I have something for you." It was our first Valentine's Day together, and I wanted it to be special. I wanted him to know that I was clean from drugs, and I was ready to start a relationship.

"Really?" he said, a bit shocked.

"Just open it."

He tore open the envelope, and the two Kings hockey tickets slipped out of the card. I was happy to see the stunned look on his face. He hadn't suspected anything, and I really pulled it off.

Two weeks later, he picked me up to take me on our first date. Even though the game was two hours away in Los Angeles, it didn't bother us much. The long ride gave us a chance to talk and get to know each other even better. He made me laugh the entire ride. It was late February, and the weather was extremely cold. As we walked to the stadium, he took my hand in his and looked down at me and smiled. It was the first time I'd felt like a normal person in a long time. I was finally stepping out of the cloud I had been in for so long. We found our seats in the stadium, and as we waited for the game to start, U2's "In the Name of Love" began to play. The song echoed all around, and I felt like a lucky girl in the middle of a romance movie. As we looked over at each other, we both understood that this was our first date.

Brian and I dated for a while, but it just didn't work out like we thought it would. I was trying my best to move on with my life and started to work at a new restaurant. Only a few days into the new job, Brian sent me flowers and a card.

I decided to clear things up by calling him. He wanted to meet, and I reluctantly agreed to see him that night at Applebee's.

When I walked into the restaurant, it was as though nothing had changed. The place was packed, and all of our old friends were still around, waiting tables and serving drinks. Brian was sitting at the bar with his back to the door. He turned around when I walked in and began to cry all over again at the sight of me. I could feel that knot of resentment inside of me melting. The place was packed, even with people we knew, and he didn't care who saw his outburst. He came over to me and pulled me into an intense hug before even saying hello. He lifted my chin and kissed me. I could feel my face growing hot and red as people eating began to stare at us.

"Why don't we go outside?"

"Yeah, maybe that's a good idea."

When we got outside, he nearly exploded with emotion. He grabbed me by the hands and looked into my eyes, "Cindy, I dreamt about us, and I just can't get it out of my head. We even had a little boy named Henry. I want you to be with me for the rest of my life. Will you marry me?" He had no ring to offer me because everything was so spontaneous, but that didn't matter to me.

"Yes. I will." Tears rolled down my face. He let me choose my own ring in the upcoming weeks. We got married on June 18, 2005.

I was still in my early 20s, and I began going out with friends after work again. I got to the point where I wasn't pursuing God, and I wasn't pursuing my husband. I was living one day at a time all over again. But despite all this, God was still pursuing me.

There was so much tension in those early years. We started trying to get pregnant, and I took on a second job at the mall. The stress only grew bigger. We couldn't get pregnant, and I constantly blamed myself for the abortion years earlier. Brian urged me to go to church with him, but when I sat in the long pews, I only felt resentment and anger toward God. I went to church, but my heart wasn't in it. All the while, I had one foot in the married life and one foot in the party life. This went on for years.

Two days before Christmas in 2008, I was working a holiday shift at the mall, which was full of Christmas shoppers. As I folded clothes on a display rack, I thought about my crumbling marriage.

As holiday shoppers hurried around me, a man and his family came in and asked me about our sales. I helped them around the store and explained the season's deals, quickly returning to my duties.

I was surprised when I felt a tap at my shoulder an hour later. I turned around to see the man and his family standing behind me.

"I'm sorry to bother you while you're working, but I really had to come back and talk to you. You know, I made it all the way to the car, and I told my family I had to come back and give this to you." He handed me a card from Champion Life Church, and my heart nearly leaped out of my chest.

"I've been to this church before," I said with excitement.

"Well, I know God put it on my heart to invite you back."

"How are things back at Champion Life? How are Damion and Zoe doing?" They were a couple I often talked to. We were both struggling through infertility issues.

"You know, it's funny you should ask," the man said. "They called me today to let me know they are pregnant."

"Wow!" I was so happy and shocked that I burst into tears. He was a sincere man, and his eyes began to water as well.

"Yeah, you probably already know how long they have been praying for this."

"Yeah, I know." Something inside of me was coming back to life just by talking to this kind man.

"My name is Tom, and my wife is Sarah. We teach the young adults service. We would love for you to come on Sunday."

"I'm so glad to meet you. I do have to get back to work, but thank you so much for inviting me." I really meant every word I told him. It was such a bizarre encounter that I knew it must be God orchestrating the whole thing. I even called Brian on my break and told him about Tom and his family.

I came home from work feeling so peaceful despite the holiday chaos. I felt as though God was continually reassuring me that the moment in the mall with Tom and Sarah was no accident. God had planned it himself. I went straight to our bedroom because I knew it was time to reconnect with God. I couldn't remember how long it had been, but the familiar peaceful feeling came over me right away.

Lord, I have spent enough time away from you. I know you are there, and I need you back in my life. Please help me. I didn't use any eloquent words, but I did cry out to

God from the pit of my soul. I took all the emotions I had been avoiding for so many years and turned them over to him.

I thought back to the day I saw Mom and Brandon together. Julie was nervously driving me to church that day to be baptized. Even Julie's mom and Jazmine were so excited for me. That day, I had made a promise to God. The important day my mom had missed was the day I declared to my friends and family that I believed in Jesus Christ. I thought it would be a new beginning, that after I had been dunked under the water I would be different and make good decisions. Instead, my family crumbled, and I ran from God.

After that, I'd forgiven Mom and Brandon because I knew that was what Jesus would do. What I'd forgotten was that Jesus offered the same forgiveness for me. I looked back on all the moments that he had tried to get my attention, but I only turned away. I understood now that Jesus was with me the night I had dumped my meth onto the concrete. He had even helped Brian and me through our relationship and our most difficult times.

I knew it was time to stop running and receive God's forgiveness. I asked him to forgive me for my broken marriage, for the abortion, for the drugs and partying — for everything. I was turning my back on all the mistakes and turning my face to God.

When I was a teenager at summer camp, Pastor Susan had explained that God reaches out to us and teaches us endurance and perseverance through hard times. I realized she was right. And that with God's help, I could endure.

I clicked on the bedside lamp and pulled out my dusty Bible. The thin familiar pages felt crisp and light as I turned to the New Testament. Nothing visible had changed, but I knew that God was already answering my prayers. I found it so amazing that no matter how far I drifted from him, God was always there for me.

I came out of the bedroom and went straight to Brian in the living room. "I need to tell you something."

Brian looked up from the TV. "Go ahead," he said after my long pause.

"I finally opened up to God and prayed. I'm ready for a change. I want to get close to him again."

He sat straight up on the couch. "This is exactly what I have been praying for. I think this is great. I have responsibilities right now at the church I'm attending, but you really should go to that church on Sunday." He jumped out of his seat and scooped me up in a hug.

Tom and Sarah went back to their church that same day and told the youth group about our meeting, and everyone prayed for me.

The very next Sunday I walked into Champion Life, and I was approached by so many people shaking my hand and introducing themselves. They talked to me like they knew me. There was something authentic about their demeanor, greeting me with true kindness and warmth. I was really thankful to God that Tom listened to God's urging and came up to me that day. His wife, Sarah, and the group constantly prayed with me, and she counseled me a great deal on becoming a better wife.

I quickly got involved with the youth ministry and found myself at church several days a week. I couldn't go a day without reading the Bible. What was even better was the fact that Brian and I were praying together. There was no more time, much less desire, to go out after work. God was moving in my life, and it was exciting. I learned that the same God who created the universe was the same God helping to heal my marriage.

The new struggle in our lives was going to two separate churches. I knew this was where God had called me. Brian felt too connected to his church family to leave. The more I urged, the more he was reluctant. However, God was still working in our marriage. After Brian listened to a CD of our youth pastor's teaching, he decided to come visit Champion Life with me one Sunday.

Brian has been at Champion Life ever since. He connected with the men's Bible study and began helping out wherever he could.

As our relationship flourished, I held on tightly to the dream of having a child. Every month that I was not pregnant was a new test of my faith. As our faith in Jesus and our involvement in church grew, so did our desire for a baby.

One day I found myself sitting on the edge of my bed looking down at two pink lines. The second line was faint, but it was there. I tried a second test with the same result. We saw a glimpse of our future forming, but it quickly faded. The next day, I began spotting, and shortly after, the doctor confirmed that I had miscarried. We grieved but trusted that God was in control. We hoped that our miracle was around the corner.

☙ ☙ ☙

The following Friday, I visited my in-laws. Brian's sister and I were sitting on the couch together when my phone rang.

"Your brother is calling you," my father-in-law said, looking down at my phone.

"Hello."

"Hey, Cindy. I hope I'm not catching you at a bad time."

"I'm just here with Brian's parents. What's up?"

"Well, I'm going to call Dad in a minute, but I wanted to tell you first. I have some news."

I joked with him, saying, "You're pregnant." I didn't really think it was possible after only being married to his wife for eight months.

"Yes! We are having a baby."

I felt like he had kicked me in the stomach, and all the air left my body. "That's great," I squeaked. Tears gushed from my face, and I held my palm to my mouth to stop from sobbing.

"I hope those are tears of joy …"

"Oh, they are. I just can't talk right now. I will call you later." They were indeed tears of joy. I was so happy that my brother was receiving this blessing. But the mending wound in my heart was ripped open. It had only been a few days since I'd miscarried.

My sister-in-law wrapped her arm around me, and I fell onto her chest and sobbed. I felt like I released every ounce of emotion with those tears. Brian walked into the room and looked stunned.

"What's going on? Did someone die?"

"No," I said, looking up at him. "My brother is having a baby." I could see by his reaction that he felt the same way I did.

"We should probably go," he said to his sister.

She took my hands in hers and squeezed them. "You're going to get through this."

I continued to sob on the way home, and Brian began to pray as he drove. Brian prayed for us and recited comforting Bible verses. My sobs turned to crying, and soon I was drying my tears. Brian pulled the car into the garage and looked over at me. "Our miracle is coming. Nothing has changed. Your brother and his wife are receiving their own little miracle, and this is such an exciting day for our family."

"I know you're right. This just really derailed me. You know, I think I want to go for a drive by myself. Just God and me."

He kissed me on the lips and took my face in his hands. "You do what you have to do."

࿐ ࿐ ࿐

As I drove alone, I turned on my worship music and soaked in the comforting words. Uncontrollable tears rolled down my face as I thought of all the barren women in the Bible that God allowed to have children. I began to whisper to God between sobs. *I know you have promised to take care of me and never leave me. I trust that you will always keep your promises.*

I'm reminded of the one thing that brings me more comfort than anything I can comprehend. Jesus wept. He didn't hide his feelings behind closed doors. He climbed up mountaintops and called out to God. When he was brutally killed, he cried out to God in front of all the people who wrongly accused him. His emotions were nothing to be ashamed of, so neither are mine. I've realized that my feelings are not weakness. I'm allowed to feel and express emotion.

My hands relaxed on the steering wheel, and I sighed. The next thought comes swiftly, like a rainstorm while the sun is shining. *God is using this pain to build my endurance.*

My pain allows me to persevere. I am still asking God for a baby. There are days when the weight of infertility brings me to my knees. But I know that God is with me and my husband, and the path God has for me is the best one. I can hear his voice, ever so faintly, reminding me: *I am strong when you are weak. Lean on me, because my yoke is easy, and my burden is light.*

THE LONG ROAD HOME
The Story of Janey
Written by Holly De Herrera

It's so dark out I hate to do it, hate to even attempt it again. But Mom taught me well enough how to get out if I needed to. Only now I can't seem to recall any of it. What did she always say to do first? I don't have time to flick through the pictures in my mind and find it, and besides, I might lose my nerve. My baby sister sleeps like she doesn't have a care in the world. I almost hate to nudge her out of whatever world she has gone to in her 6-year-old mind. I'm a year and a half older and have the weight of the world pushing down on my shoulders, like a book bag that's too heavy. A book bag filled to the brim with cement.

"Helen, get up." I say it so quietly I'm not sure I actually got my voice to tiptoe out into the open. He's always listening. And I can't risk him waking up and getting us. No, I'm sure he'll kill us for even trying again. Helen finally looks up at me, bleary-eyed and confused, a fringe of soft brown hair spread over her cheekbone. But somehow without me saying a word she knows what to do. She slips her feet into her tiny slippers, and we leave.

In just minutes we are walking down the long country dirt road that leads away from Dad's place and doesn't hold a single streetlight. It feels like it's a million miles long, and I pull Helen with me, the dark and the quiet giving the false sense of safety a little girl gets from hiding her face under the covers, even though the whole world can see her crouching there. Our feet sound loud on the gravel, so I tiptoe a little, thinking smaller feet make smaller noises.

That's when I hear them. I knew they'd be a problem. They always ruin everything. Those dogs. Why on earth doesn't that man keep his dogs locked up at night? I wonder if Dad talked to him. I wonder if he asked him to leave them out just in case we try anything. He's smart and has a way of getting what he wants. My stomach feels so tight, like Dad's belt, only tied in a knot that's spinning. I hear the dogs' chains jangling first, then their footfalls on dry grass, and soon the quiet is ripped away by their barks, so loud, like they're practically pointing a giant flashlight into our faces. Like we're criminals instead of who we actually are — children without any real hope of escape. *Why do I keep trying?*

"Come on. This way." I tug Helen's arm that dangles heavy and limp, and I encourage her with, "It's okay. I know where we can hide." Only that's a lie. Nothing looks the same in the blackness.

She only whimpers, and I resist the urge to cover her mouth with my hand. I don't have time, and besides, she's had enough of being roughed up to last a lifetime. Instead, I just squeeze my eyes shut for a second and try to remember Mom's words. *What did she say to do next? Where should we hide for the night so he won't figure it out?*

I see the dark trees of the woods, lining the edge like guardians or soldiers with no purpose but to stand there with arms arced into the blue-black sky, whispering, "Boo." *Whose side are you on, anyway? His? Do you know what kind of man he is?*

I know that my anger won't help. Besides, they're just trees, and they don't know anything. I have to stay clearheaded and brave. Helen won't know what to do if I start crying. I bite down hard on my lip before taking my first step into the ink of the woods, past the tree line. Maybe this time …

But before we have made it four steps into the woods, he appears like he was waiting there for us all along, and maybe he has been.

"Thought you could get away, did you?" His voice is so loud after all the quiet creeping and hoping, it's like glass thrown against the wall. And the horrible darkness reaches down to grab my sister and me like we're nothing at all. Like we're two tiny ragdolls with cloth for skin and painted-on triangle eyes and thin red smiles.

కారా

Mom had taught me what to do if running away became necessary, and I was obsessed with it, with doing it right, so much so that my plans would weave into my dreams. I knew every night, or most every night, I'd go down that road in my mind. Like I was practicing for a day I thought would inevitably come. Just knowing it would stalk me in my sleep made me wish I could stay up forever, but then my waking life was no better. It was the reason for the dream, after all.

Being 4 years old didn't mean I didn't know that something was wrong or that my family was different. Nothing could change it. I wished for a normal life. I wished for a kind, smiling father who made us hot cocoa and cookies and gave out warm hugs and laughter. But, no, that wasn't the way it was. Wishing was just about as useful as blowing dandelion fronds into the wind. There's no way to tell them which way to go. And wishing won't make them take root where you want them to. Especially when it seems like Dad will just find a way to crush them under his enormous boot, dug deep into the dry gravel, making them like useless pulp instead of hope.

Mom said she didn't know how she managed to always pick the wrong man. Maybe it was because she was only 16 when she and Dad married. Maybe it was because he was her only ticket out of the small cowboy town she hailed from in Oklahoma. Or maybe it was because she didn't think she deserved any better. My mom was always spunky and not one to take life lying down. I think for a little while she did, until Dad started hurting us girls. Until he put a pillow over my face and pressed it there while my little legs wiggled and kicked. He only lifted it up when he was good and ready, while I gasped for breath. That was the breaking point for Mom. But definitely not enough for him. Grandma probably resisted the urge to say I told you so. Grandma and Mom had always been a lot alike, both tiny but mighty and full of fire. Mom bought a gun after Dad ran off with me and told him that if he ever tried that again she'd shoot him dead. I tended to believe her. But for all her toughness, that didn't mean she was tough all the way down deep, where no one could see. She worked long hours, and even though we shared rent with another single mom and my uncle at one time, we barely made ends meet. Still, she did it, and we never went hungry. Not for a single day.

༚༚༚

I was 4, and Helen was 2. Uncle Joe took out the burn barrels that morning and lit the trash, and it smoldered in the barrels for a good long while, even as the sun fried anything that dared land on the sidewalk. Helen toddled out back, and we both plopped our backsides down on the back porch near an old fringy mattress. Uncle Joe didn't remember to take his matches back inside, and to me there was nothing quite as amazing as striking that long wooden match and watching the orange flame dance and flicker. Soon we began lighting the hanging strings around the mattress, and Helen and I laughed as the light danced up the threads, then sputtered out. I don't know how long we did this, but for a little while, there was nothing else in the world. Not Mom, who was taking a bubble bath in the house. Not our uncle drawing our attention away. Nothing.

The string lit again, and this time instead of dying at

the place where it met up with the mattress, it decided to take a creeping bite into the fabric. The orangey-black color moved in and dug deeper, like a leaf being devoured by a caterpillar. I dropped the matches and grabbed Helen's hand. She giggled as we slid inside the door of the house and closed it. My heart felt like it might pop right out of my chest and land on the floor in front of me, I was so scared. Maybe if I just played inside like normal and acted really good for a while it would go out and fizz away into the pale blue sky, like a bad smell. But then the black smoke began curling against the back door, climbing in through the bathroom wall where my mom was, the smell of fire getting stronger and stronger.

Mom ran out into the living room wearing a robe, with hair dripping into puddles around her feet. Good, maybe the water would help do something. But, no, not that little water up against that much smoke. Mom yelled something and grabbed a laundry basket, scooped a few clothes inside and knocked a couple pictures off the shelf into it, then scooped up Helen. Together we all ran outside, down the driveway and across the street to the sidewalk, feet splatting on pavement, down to the very end of the corner away from the house. It looked like the smoke just gobbled the house up because before I could even think to tell Mom that the whole thing was my fault, Grandma came running, looking around frantically, looking at the house and then up and down the street we weren't on and then she fainted, flat down on the sidewalk. She thought we were still in there, Mom told me later. Along with our few earthly possessions. And all I could keep wishing was that I hadn't been so irresponsible. I wished that time might rewind, go backward just one hour, and Helen and I could be sitting, playing in the sunshine with the dirt instead of with matches. This would be the one time I'd be glad my family never talked about bad stuff. Because if we didn't let our words about the sad things find their way into daylight, maybe that meant they didn't actually happen.

And that was life for us. One dark spot followed by grayish spots, then pale bluish-yellow ones. Mom remarried, and we all seemed to think this was the new start we'd always wanted, only Dad was still trying to get us and take us from Mom, and every time I'd go anywhere, Mom would explain the situation all over again. She would hold up the crumply picture she carried of my dad so they'd know to absolutely never, ever let us go with him. Then she'd go through what to do if he tried. She would play out scary stories and ask what we would do if this happened or if that happened. Where would we go and hide? Who could we call for help? The only sunshiny spots in the gray were the times we'd go to be with Grandma. She made everything good and safe. She would cook us nice meals, take us shopping and gather us up in her arms, and I just knew things were okay when we were with her. Even Dad never tried to cross Grandma.

Everyone knew and loved my grandma. "Sis," they called her. She owned a restaurant and was known for giving free meals to the hobos near the railroad tracks. I was so proud knowing she helped so many people. And I just knew she would rather die than let anything happen to her grandbabies. Somehow, with her, everything seemed right with the world. But there was always that moment when it was time to go home.

Dad managed to get custody because a mom that's hiding away and not making it to court looks more like a deadbeat than like someone doing her best to hide away from a monster. So we stayed away to avoid being put in his custody, only secretly calling Grandma once in a while to let her know we were okay.

Then he found us again, and one summer, every other week, we had to fly back to Oklahoma to stay with him and his new wife and daughter. I never could see why he tried so hard, why he wanted us with him so badly that he would hunt us down until he found us, forcing Mom and Anthony, my stepdad, to uproot again and hide. It made no sense, either, why the courts decided he was fit to have us. Everyone knew what kind of person he was.

Mom was a mess, fussing and going through the steps of what to do if he hurt us, of how to get out and where to go. By this time I was 8 and Helen was 6, and we both were smarter and stronger — still it seemed cruel to make us go there, like two tiny moths diving into the porch light, knowing full well it would burn the soft hairs of their bellies clean off.

"Ready or not, here I come!" Helen yelled.

I was hiding inside Dad's big old shed that held the washer and dryer, and Helen stepped in carefully, looking for me. It didn't take much, just the slip of her tiny foot, but she managed to knock over the powdered laundry soap, scattering tiny white granules across the wooden floorboards. Such a small thing, but that was all it took to send my stepmom, Betty, into a fit, and that night she filled Dad in on what his horrible children had done this time. I wondered what she had added to the list, because just that one thing couldn't have caused such a fuss. Or maybe it could. Maybe us just being there and being in the way was enough. I wished again and again that we could just go home and never have to come back here and never suffer the stinging belt on our behinds again. But that wasn't the case. At least not yet.

Dad came into the kitchen, picked up Helen and walked out the door that led to the yard. She was just a tiny doll in his fat hands. My stepmom yanked on my arm and pulled me to the low window looking out across the dry grass of the yard, to Dad's stocky figure walking out to the apple tree with Helen being held under her armpit. She was walking forward on small legs lifted on tiptoes to keep up with the march and stretching away from the hard pressing of his fingers under her arm. My stomach twisted and slithered, and I could feel my heart beating all the way through my body, in my face, drumming in my ears. I needed to help her! I needed to get her away, but how could I? It was my responsibility to watch over her and take care of her. My punishment was to watch, and Betty wasn't about to let me go.

Dad scooped my sister up and hooked her arms over the two "y's" in the branches, like a piglet on a spit — only her legs hung down, and her little dress dangled in the air. Birds danced in the blue sky, and butterflies darted by, up and down and clumsy, like none of nature could see that a tragedy was taking place. I wanted to run out there, lift her away from him — find a place where things like this don't happen to people so small and helpless. My baby sister was hanging in a tree, and Dad was removing his belt, and then he flung it back and slapped it hard against her peachy legs. *Whack!* The sound felt like a thin knife pushed in between my ribs. Again and again. Harder and harder. Tears slid hot down my cheeks, and I didn't care that they were dripping all over Betty's clean floor. Helen's cries filled my ears like a flood, rising higher and higher, so much that I felt I couldn't breathe.

"Stop it!" I screamed it against the windowpane. I said it again and again, but he was outside, and I was inside, and besides, he never listened to me. My stepmom pressed me against the glass so I couldn't turn away, couldn't find a place to hide and pretend my little sister was safe.

She crouched down beside me, hand still digging into my armpit, and said, "Watch, so you know that if you ever do anything bad again, you'll have the same punishment."

I wished I could scratch her eyes out of her face and scream, "Why? What have we ever done to you?" But instead I just watched as red welts rose up on Helen's legs and her buttocks tensed awaiting each blow. It seemed like hours before he took her down, before he stopped his rage, placing his hatred for the world on shoulders far too small to bear it. It seemed like hours before we were together again in the room. Helen's backside, all the way from her armpits to her knees, was black and blue and an angry red. And I knew then that there was nothing I could do to protect her. I was helpless and so full of pain in my chest, I felt I would burst into a million pieces.

The next day Mom was coming to get us. I nibbled on my nails and paced while waiting for her to come. I knew once she saw what he'd done she would hide us again. We'd move someplace, this time, I prayed, where he wouldn't find us. But darkness fell, and tensions rose. Dad had all the doors locked, and he reached up and pulled down the shades one by one, the high-pitched squeal of each one filling the quiet of the house. The lights were flicked off, and no one was to leave the house, he said. I knew then that he wouldn't just hand us over. Not this time. Flashing blue and red police lights danced in through the windows, even with the shades drawn shut. The sound of a man's voice on a megaphone telling my dad to let the kids come out and not to hurt us and to give up now before it got ugly sounded muted and weak. Maybe because we were in the house with Dad and they were all the way outside, and Dad had a gun in each hand, and he was never, ever one to give up once backed into a corner.

My stepmom just kept yelling for Dad to stop, and she

kept bawling like a cow. I almost felt sorry for her, but not really. She was a part of all this, even if she pretended not to be. Quietly, I pulled Helen and my stepsister into the closet furthest away, and together we crawled as far back into the darkness as we could, each of us making our bodies as teeny-tiny as possible. The night stretched on, and I could still hear Dad yelling and Betty begging and the megaphones pleading, but for that moment, we were safe. This is what Mom had said to do, and I felt proud for remembering and being the brave big sister. I knew she would be so happy when I told her.

Sometime in the middle of the night the closet door opened, and a police officer crouched down and said, "It's all right. You're safe now." We could see the house was dark and torn up as he was walking us through it. I just knew Dad wouldn't go down without a fight. I kept looking and craning my neck to see where he was because he was stronger than anyone else I knew and would fight every one of them off, I was just sure of it. But then I saw him, handcuffed against a squad car, then being shoved inside and the door being slammed, and I closed my eyes, knowing we had made it. We had survived the worst again.

Mom got custody, and we did what we always had: We moved away. As far away as my mom and stepdad's meager earnings could carry us. We packed up our belongings that would fit snug and tight in the 1965 Chevy Impala, and this time we moved because my uncle called and said he had found a job for Anthony and maybe this was the new start everyone needed. It was always a new start but only because we had a new place to live. Nothing really changed. Not deep down where all the blackness rested like a big old heap of mud that nobody really wanted to hear about. That's the way it was for Helen and me both, but I couldn't really just tell Mom that with all her working and trying to be superwoman and the terrible, sad way she always looked at me while pretending she had everything under control. No, we were off again, down the yellow brick road, only that road just kept doubling back on itself, over and over and over again.

I was finally in fourth grade. School was my most favorite place to be. I loved to try hard and see the proud way my teacher would look at me when she handed my test back or whatever the last assignment was. At school I could pretend I wasn't a girl with a mean dad and no real place to call home.

One day there was a substitute. She didn't know about all the warnings Mom had given. She hadn't seen the picture of Dad or been informed of what to do if he waltzed in to get me one day. And I kind of didn't mind. Some things are nice to not have the entire world know about.

I was working on something, maybe my nine times tables, I don't remember, and I had that satisfied feeling of a job well done when I let my eyes lift like a sparrow to the window of the classroom door. The tiny box, just a foot wide and a foot tall, framed my dad's thick face, peering in and staring right at me. I don't know how much time passed. I just know I couldn't move. I just sat there, holding on to my pencil, grabbing the top of the fake wood of my school desk, and thought to myself, *No matter what happens, he can't know where Helen's class is. If he finds out, that's it.*

My substitute teacher's voice shook me out from being frozen solid and said, "Your dad's here to get you, Janey. You need to go with him now."

I didn't know how to explain to her. How do you tell an adult that she's wrong? How do you explain that the person who's your dad also hurts you and might just take you and your sister home for the very last time? Something made me get up and walk to him. His dark, small eyes looked down at me as if to say, "If you say a word, you're dead."

Together we began to walk down the long hallway, his meaty fingers dug deep in my armpit like a gun — the only sound was our feet squeaking on the shiny tan tiles.

"Where is Helen's classroom? Let's go get her."

I swallowed down the burning feeling in my throat and began to walk with more purpose, being sure to keep steady and not make any sudden moves. We went down to the end of the hall that ran straight in to the principal's office. I knew that if I could only get down there, they would know what to do. Or would they?

Back home, when the police came to get Dad, they knew to bring three or four men because he was that strong, and nobody dared try to take him alone. What could a scrawny principal possibly do to my dad who knew how to hurt most anyone who crossed him? Still, I had to try. I needed to keep him away from my sister.

As soon as we got to where the hallway stretched into a T, I kicked and twisted my way out of his grip and ran into the main office. "He's here! He's here!" was all I could manage to say, but it was enough. Mom had briefed them enough times. But before anyone could try to grab Dad, he ran off. My aunt came to get Helen and me not too long after that, and all evening the adults talked in the living room about what to do.

My mom said, "He slashed the tires and cut the phone lines." Her voice sounded wobbly and far away. "Must've come here first."

We moved again. To a farm way out in the middle of nowhere. Because, I guessed, nobody would think to look there. Only I wasn't so sure.

But that was the last time Dad tried to steal us away. I don't know what changed, but it was over. And before we knew it, we'd gone years with no word from him. I started to imagine that I might actually grow up and stay in one place, and I might have some of the same teachers from one year to the next. I might actually be able to live a normal life. Maybe I would make friends, and maybe now Helen would be happy. Maybe this time things could be different, and the nightmares would end.

It was like the terrible stories of my life up to that point were buried under the earth. Nobody wanted to talk about what had happened, so we didn't. It was like Dad never even existed. We all tried to put on a smile and move forward, dragging the muck and mire of the past with us.

❧❧❧

For years, I've tried to figure out why it started, but Anthony began seeking out time alone with me and later Helen, too. I was 11, and maybe the reason was because I had started looking more like a young woman and less like a little girl. Going camping or fishing were the opportunities that made it easy for him. Later it was playing in his room when he got more comfortable and less careful. His long, thin bearded face took on a sort of sparkle, and I knew he was excited because he would get giddy, eyebrows raising up and down, trying to make it into a game. I didn't know it was wrong since he always called it "playing." Sometimes it was strip poker. Sometimes it was other things. More invasive things. At those times, I made my mind go blank. White with nothing. It was almost like I wasn't there at all.

"Come on, let's have some fun," he said, rubbing his narrow fingers up and down my back under my shirt. I played along because he asked me to, and letting people down made me feel like I was worth less than a person. Like I had no value at all if I didn't do what he asked. It really was all he asked most of the time, after all. I felt somewhere deep inside that this wasn't what love was supposed to be like, though. Love shouldn't be something you had to do, or else. Love shouldn't make your stomach hurt. At least he wanted me around. At least he didn't beat the daylights out of me every day when he got home from work.

"If you tell Mom … " He let the words dangle for me to fill in the blanks. And my mind did fill them in. I imagined all the ocean of sadness she already swam in finally just swallowing her up whole. And then she'd be gone and so would any sense of security I had. Then nobody else would know how hard she tried to give me and Helen a good life. And how she cried because she just knew that all this was her fault, anyway. Besides, I had seen firsthand that adults did what they said they'd do, when it was a punishment. No, better to remain silent. Then no one else would get hurt.

I remember one day in particular, riding my horse away from the house, the wind rippling softly through the grass and the mountains stretching all across the horizon. I just knew that there had to be a God out there that could see me. There had to be something more besides this terrible life. I let my prayer out into the quiet and imagined it flying up on the back of a bird into the cobalt-blue sky. "God, if you're real and you're up in heaven, I can't do this. I need help."

A year and a half later, Mom found out about what Anthony had been doing. Someone had told her that they suspected it, and finally, she just asked as we sat parked in front of the house one day. Since I had been taught not to lie, I just had to say it, let the words fall out of my mouth like rocks tumbling over a waterfall, finally giving way to the constant pressing and buffeting. She cried so hard I was scared she might not ever stop. I wanted to make it better, take it back, tell her, "No, he's never touched me that way. I'm fine. Really." But Mom was smart, and she had always been able to get answers. For a few months, Anthony stayed away. Then Mom finally said he could come home, but he better not even think about looking at us, hugging us or doing anything alone with us. Her eyes were always watching when he was in the house. Even with all the watching, though, I felt like a small island floating out in the middle of a black sea, alone and without any hope of being found.

High school brought with it some peace, strange to say. I thrived in school, and I loved to play basketball — any kind of sports, really. Jake came along my freshman year, and he would sit in the bleachers with my parents while I played and discuss the game, life and who knows what else. Mom loved him. Said he had something different. Even Anthony seemed to enjoy Jake's easygoing, gentle way.

"Why don't you come on over for dinner, Jake? I'm making tacos." She said it like it was filet mignon.

Jake's smile tilted to the side, and he answered, "Sounds perfect, Ma'am."

And more times than I can count, Jake ate over, and we had tacos. Before I knew it, I found my gaze catching on his face, seeing the honesty in his brown eyes, liking the way he seemed so comfortable and peaceful, taking in the way his hair fell easily around his ears, brushed his collar and swept away from his face. He'd look my way, too, and I started to see something else there. I started to see he was there for me.

Little did I know he was working at getting my parents' approval to date me. One evening we were driving in his car, and he said, "Janey, would you want to come to church with me?"

I felt safe with Jake and knew anything he suggested wouldn't hurt to try, so I answered easily and without much thought, "Sure."

I saw the smile twitch at the corner of his eye, and he turned again and added, "By the way, I hate tacos." His face erupted in a full smile, and I covered my mouth, laughing.

"What? Why didn't you say so?"

He looked over his shoulder at me, his arms crossed easily over the steering wheel. "How else was I going to get your mom to say yes to me taking you out?"

I went with Jake to church, and something about the whole thing felt so real, so stripped away of the ugliness of life, so embracing. My starving soul drank it in like a person who nearly died in the Sahara and finally came across a glistening stream. The music danced through me, a steady drumbeat stirring me to move. But it wasn't until the second time I visited that I did anything about it.

Helen and I sat at the back of the sanctuary, just observing everything. Whether we looked engaged or not, both of us felt something practically lifting us out of our seats when the pastor asked, "If any of you has never given his or her heart to the Lord, why not now?"

Jake's dad appeared, hand outstretched, and said, "Do you want to go?"

My heart hammered thick in my chest, and I felt like a person possessed with such a longing to be known, understood, loved unconditionally, made new.

I felt that cement backpack crash off my back at the realization that Jesus Christ, the Son of God, suffered along with me and hung on a tree a little like my sister had, only this tree he had willingly died on because of his love for me. This tree was stained with his blood, too, but he could have chosen to walk away from it. Only his passion to be near me compelled him to say yes to that awful suffering. And when he rose from death three days later, it was him saying, "Nothing you throw at me will defeat my love."

All the violence and cruelty was not what he wanted for me, though he had walked through it with me. He had cried with me on that dark dirt road of my dreams. Held me when my heart felt nearly broken. He was with me in that moment, in that church, and he was calling me to reach my hand back and say, "Yes. I choose to walk through whatever might come next with you." And I did. And a light filled my chest like nothing I'd ever felt before or since — now we belonged to each other, and nothing could separate me from his love. Nothing and nobody.

THE LONG ROAD HOME

༖ ༖ ༖

One thing they don't tell you about when you're young and one thing you never contemplate is sickness. I felt a fullness inside that I'd never experienced before, and I was a model student, basketball player, cheerleader and Future Business Leaders of America chapter president. My heart was at peace, despite my home life, and Jake and I were in love. It didn't take either of us long to believe we had been put together by God. And after only six months of dating, we knew we would be married someday not too far off in the distance.

The lumps in my neck seemed to appear out of nowhere my sophomore year of high school. The doctors looked so dire, so severe, as they performed more tests than I could count. Still, I didn't let them bring me down. This was nothing. I was only 16. I had my whole life ahead of me. At least, that's what I thought.

The doctor who told me seemed to mutter the diagnosis. "It's Hodgkin's Lymphoma."

The words sounded like another language, and I leaned in. "So what does that mean?" I hated the shaky way my voice sounded in the small office with its wingback chairs and too-shiny presidential desk.

"It's cancer."

"Oh."

"Stage four."

"Okay." The room was so sterile, so unfriendly. No place to realize you are most likely going to die just when you're finally happy and you want to be married and have babies and love them like you never were.

"Only 10 percent survive it."

That began my nine-month bout with surgeries, radiation and hospitalization. Jake told me later that the surgeon had pulled him aside one day and said, "So you're the boyfriend."

"Yes, sir. I am."

"Son, I know that you think you love her, but this girl is never going to amount to anything, and if she survives, she will be weak and sickly all her life. I would just go home."

Jake just said, "Thank you, sir. I'll be staying."

With a shake of his head, the man left.

Partway through my senior year, Jake and I got married. Mom and Grandma were there. Even Anthony was there, but that couldn't snatch away my joy. I had peace, come what may. I had married the man of my dreams, I felt the peace of Christ in my heart and whether I lived a day or a year or many more than that, I was finally happy.

I beat the cancer, or I should say, God beat it for me. This stunned all the nay-saying doctors, and I got the "she's lost it" look when I announced that I had been healed. Having children was out of the question, too, according to all the professionals.

"The radiation burned all of your eggs," they stated,

like they were talking about breakfast and not my dream of a family being destroyed.

But Jake and I believed God had told us they were wrong and that he would be doing the miracles to astound everyone. When I felt the off-kilter pregnancy symptoms, I wondered and went in to ask for a blood test to confirm my suspicions. My doctor told me, "You're depressed, Janey. You want so badly to have a baby, you're causing these symptoms in your body. It's impossible." I felt that old horrible weight returning. I spent weeks crying off and on, trying to pray and trust that God would get me through this, too. The symptoms didn't go away; in fact, they intensified. I begged and pleaded and finally was accepted to get the blood work, probably just to get me to shut up and confirm my deranged woman diagnosis. Only they were wrong. I was pregnant! They rushed an ultrasound and found that I was four and a half months along. The black, blotchy screen showed a baby with a heartbeat, but the little body had no legs and an oversized head.

As if to say, "See? See what you did by insisting on having babies?" the different physicians all pressed me to go across the street and have the baby aborted. What kind of life could he have? What sort of future? It would just be cruel to bring him into the world. And besides, the radiation would most likely leave him completely brain damaged.

But Jake and I believed that God didn't give us this life only to have us throw it away based on man's assessment of his or her value. "We are keeping the baby," Jake informed them, ignoring the looks of disgust thrown our way.

The day of our son's birth, six doctors were on standby for the delivery. They knew they would need the whole militia to deal with the baby's issues, if he even survived. And he did arrive, lungs crying out into the echoey, sterile room, so loud and fierce and powerful, as if to say, "Here I am! Look at me!"

There was not a single thing wrong with my boy. He was a miracle, clothed in soft fuzz. Again, God had blown away the doubts and fears with his healing hand. And still the doctors declared, "This was a fluke. It won't happen again." But again they were wrong. Our daughter was born three years later, healthy and full of life and promise.

❧❧❧

We moved our whole family, though our kids were grown adults and could have chosen to stay behind, to Palm Desert, California. Our new church here has thrived and grown from its small start with a couple of families. And we are like a huge family, walking through life together, holding each other up and rejoicing in each other's victories. I've told my story of suffering to victory wherever I go in this world, and my church knows it well.

That's why the diagnosis that came in 2010 nearly knocked us all down. It was an accident that they found it. I was in the office to get some insurance papers signed when the doctor encouraged me to get my free heart screening. They had an opening right then. I was rushed and didn't feel like it, but I did it, anyway, probably because I still didn't like to say no. In moments the tech stopped what he was doing and went out of the room. He returned, squinting at the results, concern registering like the slow lowering of a veil. The specific diagnosis came a short time later. I had Hurthle Cell Carcinoma, a rare and extremely difficult-to-treat form of thyroid cancer. Only 3 percent of thyroid cancer patients have this form of cancer, and very few survive it.

The church rallied and began to pray around the clock. Jake and I sat through endless appointments where we were given our options, but none of it seemed right. We found out about the City of Hope research hospital and applied to be considered. Because of the rarity of my cancer, I was accepted. I remember the day so clearly when we drove up to the facility. The car rolled slowly down the long stretching road, green grass spreading out and nearly glowing with its vibrancy. The facility came into view, piece by piece, as we continued on to see the sign out front, "City of Hope." It seemed to scream out to us that God was here and this was right.

I was told of my odds. Hurthle Cell isn't treatable except by surgery, as it won't absorb or be penetrated by chemotherapy or radiation treatments. So if it were to spread its burning fingers out of each tumor and into bone, other tissue or organs, there was no hope of survival. There were seven tumors, and only surgery would tell if I would live or die. But I knew that wasn't true. Only God would tell, and I believed he was saying, "Trust me."

After the surgery, the doctor entered the room. "We've never seen anything like this before. Two of the tumors were infected, but they didn't spread from one to the other. They were growing simultaneously and completely independent of each other, but not spreading outside of the walls of each tumor. So we were able to remove them, and we believe you will survive." I have been cancer free ever since.

Jake and I have clung to God's word throughout our marriage and can see the evidence of the words in Romans 8:28: "And we know that in all things God works for the good of those who love him, who have been called according to his purpose." And he has.

My God worked everything, even the suffering, gaping, ugly parts of my life, and wove it into a story that has reached its hands out to touch souls in places I will never know or see on this side of heaven.

I don't have the nightmares anymore, though I did all the way into my 30s. These days the long, dark paths don't scare me. Neither do lurking shadows or dogs barking up against a chain-link fence. I walk my path with Christ and know that with him, I am never alone. No matter how big and angry the enemy, God always gives me strength to carry on.

UNRESOLVED
The Story of Phil
Written by Marty Minchin

The hospital hallway, glowing with fluorescent lights, stretched into eternity.

My feet dragged with the weight of loneliness, and I looked down at the linoleum floor. It seemed like everyone was watching as I trekked toward the exit. Nurses, orderlies, patients' family members. Did they all know my story?

Behind me was my wife, who had died in my arms in the dark quiet of the early morning. The sounds of her gasping final breaths echoed in my ears. When she'd finally let go, I'd rested my head on the side of her bed and sobbed.

Cancer took her before her 30th birthday.

I pushed open the glass door to exit the hospital and stepped out into the eerie silence of the night. It hardly ever snowed in Tacoma, Washington, but the air was filled with swirling flakes. I looked up at the dark sky, up into the endless universe.

Why?

All I heard was silence.

෴ ෴ ෴

I'd known loneliness since I was a kid. I was born in Fort Benning, Georgia, but we moved every year until I was in third grade. My parents provided for me, but otherwise they were distant, and my dad, who was an alcoholic, was entrenched in a routine of nightly drunkenness. My only sibling, a sister, is 10 years younger than me. We were never close.

School didn't interest me, even when we settled down long enough to establish some kind of normalcy. The classroom was the last place I wanted to be, and in junior high, I quickly fell into the drugs and party scene. I smoked marijuana every day, and all I wanted to do was go out and have fun. If I had to name a favorite subject, it would be music — I didn't want to play an instrument, but I listened to any record I could buy.

I partied my way into high school, where I played football, ran track and hardly looked at a book. One lazy afternoon at a friend's house my senior year, however, Sue walked in the door, and my life changed.

The guys were lounging around smoking dope when the door opened. My friend John's girlfriend came in, followed by a slender girl with blondish-brown hair and a great big smile. I sat up and tried not to stare. She had pretty brown eyes and a cute pug nose that wiggled when she talked. *Who is this girl? I wonder if she will go out with me?*

Unfortunately, I was way too shy to ask her directly. I was a known party guy, albeit a quiet one, and she didn't do drugs, smoke or drink. She was a straight-A student at the rival high school. I didn't even know if I would manage to graduate.

Instead of talking to her, I meandered around the situation and finally mustered up the courage to ask John to ask his girlfriend to ask Sue if she'd be willing to go on a double date.

I almost fell over when her answer made it back through the system.

She said yes.

Our first few dates were as low-key as I was. We hung out at her house or mine, and soon we were going to drive-ins and settling into conversations that stretched into hours but felt like minutes. Under her bubbly, friendly-but-shy personality and my loner veneer were two souls searching for answers. She was 18, and her mother was dying of cancer. With high school graduation looming, I wrestled with whether to go to college, join the military or establish myself as a long-term bum.

I could feel myself changing a little as Sue and I got closer, although I still broke free to hang out with the guys for smokes and a couple of drinks when I could. Over time, my group of guy friends dwindled to one, but that was enough to maintain my habits on the side. Sue had her opinions about my extracurricular activities, but I tried not to do them around her, even though smoking two and a half packs a day was hard to pull off without lighting up in front of her. At least I tried not to smoke in the car.

I managed to barely earn that high school diploma, but

it didn't have much impact on my life. After graduation, Sue moved into an apartment and began attending school to be a dental assistant. My room at my parents' home seemed fine, so I stayed put and worked here and there — just enough to pay for gas and going out. Sue and I kept dating, but I was taking my relationship with her about as seriously as I was everything else in my life.

Life was getting very serious for Sue, however. She had grown up in a family that went to a church that didn't put much stock in doctors. When Sue's mother finally went to a doctor and was diagnosed with breast cancer, the disease was well progressed. She only lived a month more.

Sue didn't talk to me much about it, which was okay because I really didn't know what to say, anyway. I had no idea how to handle the situation or how to make Sue feel better. I didn't even go to the funeral. The tragedy forced us to look for substance in our relationship, and when we couldn't find it, she broke up with me.

Not a big deal, I told myself. I'd told her I'd loved her once when I was drunk, but she'd never said it back to me. The breakup would be like a hangnail: annoying, but the little pain there was wouldn't last long. *I'll find someone else next week.*

That someone else never materialized for me, but Sue soon moved on to another guy. Her new relationship didn't sit too well with me, so I called her up one night.

"Seriously?" she replied, when I suggested we rekindle our romance. "You need to grow up!"

"That's fine. I get it." I knew she was right.

We hung up. A day later, though, my unhappiness felt a little heavier. *This isn't good.* I called her back.

This time, she stayed on the line and talked. Soon, we were going out, and I moved in with her. My buddies started hanging out at the apartment on the weekends, drinking and smoking pot with me when Sue was gone, but I could tell she didn't like it.

She'd stopped going to church when her mom died, which was fine with me. I had no interest in church, and I didn't want those weird people exerting any influence over Sue. If she started attending church on the weekends, before you know it she'd be there on Tuesdays and Wednesdays, too.

Six months into our new living arrangement, Sue announced that she'd had enough. I could see the church influence seeping into her head.

"Hey, look. Either we get married or you have to move out. We can't live together anymore. I like you, and I'll still date you, but this isn't right."

Then she threw out the kicker.

"If you really love me, you'll marry me."

I knew it was coming. I wanted to marry Sue, but I knew if we got married, I'd have to get serious and get a real job. I'd have to grow up.

I gave her ultimatum a good long thought. She wasn't asking me to do something I didn't want to do. She was just asking me to do it sooner than I wanted.

"All right," I finally conceded. "Let's get married. I'll get a real job."

And I did. An upholstery shop hired me, and Sue and I got married at the justice of the peace. Her coworkers at the dental practice threw us a wedding party at one of their houses. We celebrated with her grandmother and aunt and my parents and sister, along with Sue's coworkers. After a honeymoon in Seattle, we moved from the apartment to a log cabin. When Sue got pregnant, we settled into half of her grandmother's duplex.

I was pretty happy about the baby, although it was just another indicator that I needed to grow up and get a better job. Sue was thrilled.

Amy was born with the umbilical cord wrapped around her neck, and she came out blue due to lack of oxygen. We didn't realize it had affected her until she was 9 months old. She stopped rolling over from her stomach to her back, and she couldn't sit up or focus. Doctors kept telling us, "This is wrong," but we figured it would work itself out.

Finally, a doctor laid out Amy's condition for us. He told us Amy had autism, cerebral palsy and a bunch of other words that were a mile long that I didn't understand. She'd be severely disabled.

Considering the news, we took it pretty well. I didn't know what to do other than accept it. Sue seemed to handle it on the outside, but she never told me how she felt deep down. By then, I'd gotten a job with the railroad driving spikes, and I started traveling up and down the West Coast working on the rails. Sue was left at home to take care of Amy.

One day, Sue dropped the news on me that she was going back to her mom's church.

"No, you're not. That's crazy." *Why in the world would she want to go back to that weird place?*

"I feel a calling to go back to church," she explained. "I don't care if you want me to or not. I feel like God wants me to go back to church."

"Where did this come from?"

She just looked at me.

"Okay. Go back. I don't care."

The problem was, I did care. I finally concluded that the only way to get her to stop going to church was to go with her and see what this place was all about. With my long hair and beard, they'd probably kick me out, anyway, and Sue would see just how kooky they were.

A month later, I dropped my own bombshell. "Next week, I'll go to church with you," I told my wife.

Her jaw dropped. "Why?"

"I just want to check it out."

Church wasn't what I'd expected. As soon as I walked through the door, people introduced themselves and shook my hand. They didn't seem to care how I looked. They seemed to be glad I was there. I had never experienced such acceptance, and there was no mistaking the happiness shining from Sue's eyes when she was at church.

There has to be something to this.

I didn't know anything about God, but since I was a little boy, I'd felt he was with me. When my dad was serving a tour in Vietnam, I talked to God every night and asked for my dad to come home safely. I didn't understand God, but I believed he was watching over me. At church, God became clearer. I began to understand that I could have a friendship with him and that he wanted to forgive me for bad things I'd done.

Without realizing it, I'd been primed my whole life to get to know God, and at church we finally were introduced. Within two months of setting foot in the church building, I was baptized and helping out with the church's ministries.

Life just got better and better. I was making more money at my job, and Sue and I saved up and bought our first house. Even with the challenges of taking care of Amy, we had a happy marriage. We had plenty of support from our family and friends, and if we ever wanted a night off, we had a roster of babysitters to call.

When Sue told me she was pregnant again, I worried that we'd have another disabled child. She kept asking me why I was so anxious because she was sure the baby was fine. Sue was right.

While I was getting more involved in the church, I held onto my pot habit. My favorite place to smoke was the roof, but when my second daughter got old enough to talk she ratted me out. It took Sue about two seconds to figure out what was going on when Rachel asked her, "Why is Daddy on the roof?"

I decided I was done. I didn't want to set that example for my kids. I was moving up in my career at the railroad, and smoking pot was no longer acceptable there, either. I quit cold turkey.

Life, I regularly reminded myself, was very, very good.

Then Sue started coughing.

જાજાજ

She couldn't shake her cold, so I took her to a doctor. He diagnosed her with the flu, and she got better after taking the medicine he prescribed. When the cough returned, the doctor gave her the same medicine and assured us she was fine.

That October, we bundled the kids into the car and drove six hours to Spokane, Washington, for a church conference. We settled into a nice room in a hotel, ready for five days of hanging out with friends and going to meetings.

"I don't feel well," Sue told me three days into the conference. "I want to go home."

I knew she'd been struggling, so I didn't protest. We repacked the car and drove the six hours back, stopping only to drop the kids off with my mom before heading to the urgent care clinic. The drop-in medical center in a strip mall was one of the few places open on a Sunday that we knew would take our insurance.

The doctor on duty did a simple X-ray, and when he returned with the negative of Sue's chest, his expression said it all.

"There's a quarter-size spot on one of her lungs," he

said, pointing to the big black dot on the X-ray. "You need to see a specialist."

Sadly, from then on, her condition only got worse.

న్నన్నన్న

The next day, a doctor stuck a long needle in Sue's back and determined that she had progressive lung cancer.

"How is that possible?" I asked, incredulous that my wife, who'd never smoked a day in her life, had this disease. I'd smoked a lot myself, but never around her.

We got sucked into a brutal cycle of treatment and attempts at recovery. An oncologist would pump Sue full of chemotherapy drugs, and afterward, she'd lie in bed growing weaker by the day.

I kept working, and every night I'd come home to find my house full of people from the church, which didn't believe in doctors. I'd kick them out and tell them not to come back — they were there to help, but I wasn't on board with their beliefs about health and healing.

Finally, my mom agreed to help us out on a regular basis, and I allowed two women from church to stay during the day. At night, I'd sit with Sue. Her downhill slide never hit any bumps, curves or rough spots that might slow it down.

When she became so weak that she couldn't move, doctors told her that the chemotherapy wasn't working, and she needed massive radiation. An MRI showed the cancer had spread all over her body. But one week of treatment was all she could absorb. I checked her into the hospital to recuperate in early February.

All along, I'd never doubted that God would heal Sue. I would understand if he struck me dead. I felt like I might deserve that. A good God, however, would never take someone like Sue. I prayed. I fasted, going without food to help me better focus on prayer. We prayed together. In her heart, though, I think Sue knew she was going to die. In my heart, I was convinced God was going to bring her back to health.

On her fourth night at the hospital, I dozed off in a chair. Sue's aunt woke me around midnight with a gentle shake.

"I think it's time."

I sat by her bed, holding her the best I could. The hours dragged into the early morning, and the space between Sue's ragged breaths widened. When the last space grew into what seemed like forever, I waited for God to bring her back to life.

He didn't. And I didn't know what to do.

I sat there by her bed, trying to say the goodbye I wasn't prepared for. My wife was only 29 years old.

"Phil, it's time to leave," the doctor said quietly. I had no clue what to do.

I gathered my coat and hat and wandered out of the hospital room into the hallway, where a gauntlet of stares greeted me.

I had to accept her death, but I didn't accept it. *Are you kidding me? What am I going to do now? Our 8 year old thinks her mom was sick with a cold, and now I have to tell her that Sue is dead.*

Sue had possessed a great faith and had always told me not to worry. What else could I think? As freezing snowflakes peppered my face in the hospital parking lot, I had to face the truth. My wife was gone.

ॐ ॐ ॐ

I held myself together through the blur of the funeral, but when space opened up for me to think, it quickly filled with anger.

Why would God take her? I'm the one who lived a party lifestyle, and I probably should have died nine times by now. Where is the justice in this?

There also was the problem of how I would take care of our daughters, one of whom needed constant care. I didn't know how to dress them, bathe them or braid their hair. How would I know what clothes to pick out? My girls looked up to me. How would I ever provide for them and take care of them without my wife? Without *their mom*?

I channeled my fury straight at God. I was mad at him. I was mad at myself. I kept going to church, but I pulled back from participating. It was all I could do to show up. Eventually, a beer sounded a lot better than the hard seat of a church pew.

One night, when all hope seemed to have buried itself in the ground with Sue, I decided to drink myself to death. I'd limited my drinking to a six-pack at a time up until then, but when I pulled in the parking lot of the bar down the road, I left my limitations in the car. I settled in at the bar and started ordering drinks.

Hours, maybe many hours, later, I fumbled around the parking lot, feeling for the lock on my car. I jammed the key at it, but it wouldn't fit.

Hmmm. Maybe my car's over there. My car seemed to look like all of the other cars, and no matter how many locks I tried, I couldn't get the right one.

"Sir, we're going to have to call the police." I forced my eyes toward the bar's security guard.

Phone call. I need to make a phone call.

Two days earlier, a young man at church had joined the throngs of people offering help I didn't want. I'd talked to him at church a few times. He knew the pain I was going through.

"Here's my number," he said, holding out a white slip of paper. "If you ever need anything, just call me."

I jammed the paper in my wallet. *Yeah, right. I don't need anything from you.*

"Thanks," I said, happily turning my back on yet another do-gooder.

The security guard wasn't backing off.

"Please, can I make a phone call? Just one call." The guard walked me to a phone in the bar, and I called that young man. He drove me home, put me in bed and somehow found my car at a bar a quarter mile from the parking lot I'd ended up in. The next day, doctors hooked me up to a bunch of IVs and then sent me home to sleep it off. I parked myself on the couch, watching the daylight fade into evening.

Who do you think you are that you can judge me and question my ideas?

I was sure I was hearing God's voice. He had a lot to say.

I give life, and I take life. I do what I want, not what you want.

A sense of God's presence filled that room that had felt so empty. I knew he was there, explaining, yet not explaining, who he was. My questions weren't being answered, but suddenly the answers didn't seem so pressing.

It was time for me to shape up and move on. My love for God felt like a boulder under my feet, far too big to ever move. I knew that God would never abandon me, and his love and care for me would be the foundation of my life.

I don't know why Sue died instead of me. I don't know why the moon rises and the sun sets, either. It wasn't my place to know. God wasn't going to tell me, but he was going to take care of my daughters and me.

Big changes had come abruptly in my life. I fell for Sue the first time I saw her. I gave up smoking pot in a day. And from that night on, I never worried again. I trusted completely that God knew what he was doing with my life.

అఄఄ

There was plenty of reason to worry, however. Foremost was the $70,000 in hospital bills from Sue's treatments and hospital stays. I didn't have much in savings, and the church had pitched in for her funeral costs.

I sat down one day and wrote to every doctor, specialist, surgeon and hospital I owed. Each letter outlined the amount of the bill and how much I could afford to pay every month based on 25 to 30 years of payments.

Two weeks later, their replies began arriving. The response was universal: The bill was paid off. I owed nothing.

I knew right then that God was taking care of me. Those letters were no coincidence. Nothing good had happened up to that point, and as those letters piled up, I began to understand that Sue's death would not be the end of our world.

My mother said she'd help me out with the girls and the house for a year, granting me 365 days to pull it together. My daughters had adored their mother — she was their hero. I hadn't been as involved in their lives — I was just their dad. My father was an alcoholic, and he hadn't been the best role model, but it was time for me to learn how to be a real father.

We began trickling back into church life, and a friend there decided to turn matchmaker on me. She invited me and another woman from church, who I'd never talked to, to dinner at her house one night. I brought Rachel, and she brought her kids. There was no spark between any of us, but during our conversation it came up that Diane was looking for a job. The clock was ticking on my mom's offer, so I told Diane I could pay her to stay with Amy eight hours a day while I was at work.

"It will be a lot of work," I warned. "You probably don't want to do it."

To my surprise, Diane called me the next day. She was willing to try the job, and I said, "Sure." I'd see her every evening when I came home from work, and our daily chitchat grew into hours-long conversations. We secretly started dating, but I didn't want to tell anyone right away. I even made her sit on the other side of the church from me. One day she strode in and sat right next to me, to everyone's surprise.

I had sworn never to get married again because I felt it was too risky. Our kids didn't like each other, but we figured out how to work through it. We were married in December.

ॐॐॐ

Eventually, I was able to buy a house big enough so that every kid could have a bathroom. Our Brady Bunch family wasn't always so rosy, and the kids could fight like cats and dogs. At my 40th birthday at the new house, some friends of mine casually mentioned that I should check out the local mega-church. Our church had 500 people; this one regularly drew 6,000 on a Sunday.

We pulled into the parking lot, which sat in the shadow of the church's huge dome.

"I can't go in there," I told Diane. "I'm going to stand out. It will be too uncomfortable."

She raised an eyebrow. "How are you going to stand out with all those people? Are you done with excuses? Let's go in."

The music, performed by a full band, hit me in the face when I walked in the door. I'd spent years singing out of a hymnal while the church pianist played.

"Wow." I loved it. "This is where I want to go."

We allocated six months to transition to our new church and ensure that our leadership roles were filled before we left the old church. At this new church, there was no pressure to wear a suit. We quickly made more friends than I'd ever had. Best of all, this church allowed the Spirit of God to move freely and without restriction. People were laying their hands on each other and asking God for help on behalf of their friends. Others spoke in a special language when they felt the Spirit of God inspire them. I had never known God like this before.

I did lay down one rule with my wife at our new church: No more children's ministry. I had labored for years working with kids at the old church, and I was done. I refused to even set my foot in the children's area at the new church.

Diane, however, volunteered immediately. One Sunday she asked me to bring her a Coke between Sunday church services while she stayed with the kids' class.

"I'll meet you at the door. I'm not going in."

She wasn't waiting at the door, forcing me to walk into the children's building to find her. She was stranded with a group of kids and no adult helper.

"Can you stay?" I shook my head.

"Please? The other leader didn't show up. I need help."

Three weeks later, I was the class leader, and a few years later, I was in charge of the whole elementary children's department. The ministry was just fun. For years I had worked with five or 10 kids each Sunday, and at this church several hundred attended Sunday children's services. We had our own band and a soundboard, and leaders taught kids and performed skits and songs. The kids were having a blast, and so was I.

☙☙☙

As I moved up in my career at the railroad, I was able to take our family to Palm Springs for vacation every year. We'd rent a house for a week, and I'd often let each kid bring a friend. On a trip seven years ago, we began to feel as if God might want us to consider living in California.

My company didn't have an office in Southern California, and without a place to work, any move would be a no-go. "If this is what you want," we told God, "you make the impossible happen."

However, the railroad company merged with another company, expanding our work on the West Coast. My Blackberry buzzed during a meeting one afternoon to alert me to a new in-house job posting — near Los Angeles.

I texted Diane.

Go for it, she replied.

After the meeting, I met with several guys from out of town who were working on house construction in Washington. When I mentioned the job opening, one of them piped up that he'd once been in charge of the railroad's California territory. He couldn't assure me of the job, but he could get me an interview.

I flew down and interviewed, but I didn't hear anything for two weeks — enough time for me to convince myself I wanted it, badly. After a particularly bad day at work, I sat in my office overcome with longing to get to California. The phone's ring startled me in the dark room. The job was mine, and the start date was months earlier than I'd planned.

"I don't know how I'm going to make this happen," I said to Diane. "We need to sell our house."

"It's already happening," she reminded me. We asked God to put things in place for our move.

We put our house up for sale, and when no buyers responded, the company purchased it. The company moved us and provided generously for our expenses. We were riding a train that I couldn't have stopped if I'd had my hand on the brake. Before I knew it, we'd bought a house in Palm Springs with a pool that was soon filled with grandkids.

One of our first orders of business was to find a church. From people we knew in Tacoma, we learned about a new church in Palm Desert called Champion Life Church. It had opened a year before with five people, and more than 200 were attending when we got there. Diane and I jumped right in. In the seven years we've been there, we've participated in a number of Life Groups, where small groups of people meet regularly for Bible study and socializing, and we've taught new member classes. The church's motto is, "Don't do life alone," and we've found that to be true as our lives have filled with friends from Champion Life. The church has also helped us strengthen our connection with God, as we've learned so much from Champion Life's focus on talking to God through prayer.

ॐॐॐ

I still don't know why Sue died. But God has taken care of me every step of the way since. Diane and I have been married for 24 years. We take care of Amy, who is now 33, at home, and we use the stories of God's work in our lives to inspire others and teach them about the amazing transformations God can bring about in people's lives.

I recently stood in a soccer stadium in the poorest state in Honduras. Praise music swelled into the arena where thousands of local people packed into the seats. It was the smallest soccer stadium in the country, but it had been built brick by brick by a man who had a dream and the gumption to knock on doors and ask for money. He wanted the stadium's first use to be for God.

That's why we were there.

The One Nation, One Day crusades were happening simultaneously in all 18 Honduran states. I've joined a national mission team, where I talk about how God has worked in my life, and help train Christian leaders, but on this day I was there to pray and ask God to heal people.

Through my prayers and the prayers of others, I saw people healed of all kinds of ailments. I saw people dedicate their lives to following God.

Years ago, as I lay on the couch in despair, God asked me why I doubted him.

I don't doubt anymore. God has taken care of me in ways that I could never have imagined.

Now, I simply marvel at his greatness.

CONCLUSION

My heart is full. When I became a pastor, my desire was to change the world. My hope was to see people encouraged and the hurting filled with hope. As I read this book, I saw that passion being fulfilled. However, at Champion Life Church, rather than being content with our past victories, we are spurred to believe that many more can occur.

Every time we see another changed life, it increases our awareness that God really loves people and he is actively seeking to change lives. Think about it: How did you get this book? We believe you read this book because God brought it to you seeking to reveal his love to you. Whether you're a man or a woman, a businessman or a waitress, blue collar or no collar, a parent or a student, we believe God came to save you. He came to save us. He came to save them. He came to save all of us from the hellish pain we've wallowed in and offer real joy and the opportunity to share in real life that will last forever through faith in Jesus Christ.

Do you have honest questions that such radical change is possible? It seems too good to be true, doesn't it? Each of us at Champion Life Church warmly invites you to come and check out our church family. Freely ask questions, examine our statements and see if we're "for real" and, if you choose, journey with us at whatever pace you are comfortable. You will find that we are far from perfect. Our scars and sometimes open wounds are still healing, but we just want you to know God is still completing the process of authentic life change in us. We still make mistakes in our journey, like everyone will. Therefore, we acknowledge our continued need for each other's forgiveness and support. We need the love of God just as much as we did the day before we believed in him.

If you are unable to be with us, yet you intuitively sense you would really like to experience such a life change, here are some basic thoughts to consider. If you choose, at the end of this conclusion, you can pray the suggested prayer. If your prayer genuinely comes from your heart, you will experience the beginning stages of authentic life change, similar to those you have read about.

How does this change occur?

Recognize that what you're doing isn't working. Accept the fact that Jesus desires to forgive you for your bad decisions and selfish motives. Realize that without this forgiveness, you will continue a life separated from God and his amazing love. In the Bible, the book of Romans, chapter 6, verse 23 reads: "The result of sin (seeking our way rather than God's way) is death, but the gift that God freely gives is everlasting life found in Jesus Christ."

Believe in your heart that God passionately loves you and wants to give you a new heart. Ezekiel 11:19 reads: "I will give them singleness of heart and put a new spirit within them. I will take away their stony, stubborn heart and give them a tender, responsive heart" (NLT).

CONCLUSION

Believe in your heart that "if you confess with your mouth that Jesus is Lord and believe in your heart that God raised him from the dead, you will be saved" (Romans 10:9 NLT).

Believe in your heart that because Jesus paid for your failure and wrong motives, and because you asked him to forgive you, he has filled your new heart with his life in such a way that he transforms you from the inside out. Second Corinthians 5:17 reads: "When someone becomes a Christian, he becomes a brand new person inside. He is not the same anymore. A new life has begun!"

Why not pray now?

Lord Jesus, if I've learned one thing in my journey, it's that you are God and I am not. My choices have not resulted in the happiness I hoped they would bring. Not only have I experienced pain, I've also caused it. I know I am separated from you, but I want that to change. I am sorry for the choices I've made that have hurt myself, others and denied you. I believe your death paid for my sins, and you are now alive to change me from the inside out. Would you please do that now? I ask you to come and live in me so that I can sense you are here with me. Thank you for hearing and changing me. Now please help me know when you are talking to me, so I can cooperate with your efforts to change me. Amen.

HOPE IS RISING

The Coachella Valley's unfolding story of God's love is still being written … and your name is in it.

I hope to see you this Sunday!

Pastor Eddie Windsor
Champion Life Church
Palm Desert, California

Don't Do Life Alone.

We would love for you to join us at Champion Life Church!

We meet Sunday mornings at 10 a.m. at
72745 Highway 111, Palm Desert, CA 92260.

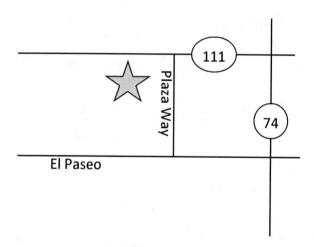

Please call us at 760.835.3700 for directions,
or contact us at www.championlifechurch.com.

For more information on reaching your city with
stories from your church, go to
www.testimonybooks.com.

GOOD CATCH
PUBLISHING

Did one of these stories touch you?
Did one of these real people move you to tears?
Tell us (and them) about it on our Facebook page at
www.facebook.com/GoodCatchPublishing.